HOW TO GUIDE
GIRL SCOUT CADETTES ON

BREATHE

IT'S YOUR PLANET—LOVE IT! A LEADERSHIP JOURNEY

A Girl Scout leadership journey invites girls to explore a theme through many experiences and from many perspectives.
All the joys of travel are built right in: meeting new people, exploring new things, making memories, gathering keepsakes. This guide is your suitcase.
It's packed with everything you need for a wonderful trip that will change girls' lives.

Girl Scouts of the USA

girl scouts

PHOTOGRAPHS
Page 17: courtesy of National
Renewable Energy Laboratory;
Page 44: NASA/courtesy of
nasaimages.org; **Pages 90, 92:**
courtesy of Miwa Koizumi.

The women mentioned in this
book are examples of how
women have used their voice
in the world. This doesn't mean
that GSUSA (or you) will agree
with everything they have ever
done or said.

SENIOR DIRECTOR, PROGRAM RESOURCES:
Suzanne Harper

ART DIRECTOR: **Douglas Bantz**

WRITER: **Anne Marie Welsh**

CONTRIBUTORS: **Toi James, David Bjerklie,
Kate Gottlieb, Kathleen Sweeney, Valerie Takahama**

ILLUSTRATORS: **Talitha Shipman, Hannah Stouffer**

DESIGNER: **Alexander Isley Inc.**

EXECUTIVE EDITOR, JOURNEYS: **Laura Tuchman**

GSUSA DESIGNERS: **Sarah Micklem, Rocco Alberico**

STATEMENT OF TRUST

Girl Scouts of the USA creates national program materials to serve our vast and diverse community of girls. To help bring topics "off the page and into life," we sometimes provide girls—and their volunteers—with suggestions about what people across the country and around the world are doing, as well as movies, books, music, web pages, and more that might spark girl interest.

At Girl Scouts of the USA, we know that not every example or suggestion we provide will work for every girl, family, volunteer, or community.

In partnership with those who assist you with your Girl Scout group, including parents, faith groups, schools, and community organizations, we trust you to choose "real life topic experts" from your community, as well as movies, books, music, websites and other opportunities that are most appropriate for the girls in your area and that will enrich their Girl Scout activities.

Thank you for all you do to bring the Girl Scout Leadership Experience to life with girls, so that they become leaders in their own lives—and the future leaders the world needs!

CONTENTS

"**Fresh air** is your great friend."

Come on in and *Breathe* a While!

Breathing is at the center of life. Billions of living things breathe every moment of every day.

That's why *Breathe* calls on Cadettes across the country and around the world to use their leadership skills and values to protect the air of Planet Earth. The journey invites girls to engage their minds and hearts as they explore air with all their senses. All along the way, they will be encouraged to reach for those moments of sparkling clarity that a breath of fresh air can bring. They will also be invited to use their flair—in everything they do.

What the girls learn about air, and the curiosity that this new knowledge inspires, will be the springboard to caring about our planet now and throughout their lives. The Cadettes and you are joining an enduring tradition. The wonders of the natural world and the need to care for them have been at the core of Girl Scouting since its founding in 1912.

Fresh air has always been integral to Girl Scouting. It was something Girl Scouts founder Juliette Gordon Low loved. A drive in the open air, in her "motor," as she liked to say, was something she thought indispensable to health and well-being. She knew that air, and all that helps keep it pure, had to be protected. "For in this United States of ours," she said, "we have cut down too many trees and our forests are fast following the buffalo." That's the spirit of this journey, too: Fresh air is something to seek out, protect, and cherish.

Reaching for the Senses, and Flair!

To engage the Cadettes in the many aspects of air, this journey calls into play all the senses. Air isn't just smelled; it's seen and heard. Often it can be felt, and tasted, too.

As the Cadettes use all of their senses to become aware of air issues in their region, and in the larger world, they'll also become aware of their flair. Flair is something everyone has, even if she's not yet attuned to it. Making the most of their flair can make girls effective in teamwork, and in public speaking. That translates into being effective at educating and inspiring others to care about air.

In this way, the journey engages girls in developing into leaders who understand the importance of air and why it must be cherished, and who can also move forward to make a difference in any arena they choose.

HEARTS AND MINDS

So much information is now available about environmental problems facing our planet and what must be done to correct them. *Breathe* is part of a series of Girl Scout leadership journeys that invites girls, and their families and adult volunteers, to make sense of that information so they can act for the betterment of Earth.

The umbrella theme for the series—*It's Your Planet—Love It!*—came directly from a brainstorm with teen Girl Scouts. Its sentiment is clear: The desire to nurture and protect is first and foremost an act of love. If girls love Planet Earth and all its wonders—airy and otherwise—they will naturally be moved to protect it. Love for Planet Earth is the true and necessary starting point for thoughtful and sustained environmental action.

YOU'RE ON THIS JOURNEY, TOO!

As you guide girls to Take Action to protect the world's air, you may find yourself adjusting some of your own air habits. If you do, you'll be adding to the air currents the girls create. And you'll see that when you work to create fresher air across the world, every little breeze counts!

You may already be deeply committed to environmental causes—or not. Either way, you will be guiding girls on a journey of learning and doing that creates larger air currents in their lives and in the world.

All along its airy route, *Breathe* engages girls in science, math, the outdoors, and environmental stewardship. You may be an expert in one or all of these areas—or none. No matter—there's no need to have all the answers! All you need to guide your group of Cadettes is right here in this book. Just add your own sense of wonder, and an eagerness to explore all that air offers and accomplishes.

Imagine the power of nearly 400,000 Cadettes and their volunteers and families making choices that conserve and protect Earth's air. What are you waiting for? Take flight!

NEED TO CLEAR THE AIR?

As the Cadettes team up to clear Earth's air, they may find themselves wanting to clear their own air space. That means all the relationships around them. *aMAZE: The Twists and Turns of Getting Along*, the premier Girl Scout leadership journey for Cadettes, offers plenty of air-clearing strategies.

Snapshot of the Journey

SESSION 1

**Blare
in the Air!**

Girls focus on the sense of hearing as they explore both the noise people routinely create and the sounds of silence and nature. Girls begin to consider:

- how what they value can influence how they care for Earth's air
- the importance of making silent time for themselves

SESSION 2

Scent Sense

Girls explore how various scents make them feel. They begin to consider:

- relaxation techniques
- why their AWAREness of air matters

SESSION 3

What's in the Air?

Girls investigate the science of air. They use what they have learned to:

- create an air-quality observation tool
- deepen their AWAREness of the importance of caring for air

SESSION 4

Get AWARE

Girls observe and record air-quality issues at their chosen location. They also consider:

- the special flair each girl brings to the team
- their own reasons for caring about air

SESSION 5

**ALERT Who
About What?**

Girls earn their AWARE Awards and:

- share their personal reason for caring about air
- make a team choice about an ALERT project to engage others in caring for air

SESSION 6

**Inspiration,
Please!**

Girls plan the specifics of their ALERT project, including:

- identifying an Air Care Team
- choosing how they will influence the team to act for air

SESSION 7 ALERT! It's Happening!	Girls put their ALERT project in motion by: • using what they know to educate and inspire an Air Care Team to act
SESSION 8 Take the Pulse	Girls earn their ALERT Awards and consider the impact of their efforts. They: • develop ideas to AFFIRM the results of their actions and pass them on to Girl Scout Juniors • enjoy "Air Time" activities
SESSION 9 Signs of AFFIRMation	Girls create their AFFIRMation collage and a special note about it for Girl Scout Juniors. They also: • earn the AFFIRM Award • finish "Air Time" fun • plan their Closing Celebration
SESSION 10 Up, Up, and Away!	Girls celebrate their accomplishments on this journey and as Heirs Apparent of air and all Earth's elements.

Friends and Family Network

It's great for Cadettes to have a wide network of people in their lives. Reach out and see how parents, aunts, grandmothers, cousins, and other relatives and family friends can be involved in the journey. They might pitch in on the girls' ALERT project or suggest guest speakers or field trips. They may have a craft expertise to share. Or they may want to assist in planning celebrations and ceremonies—or support the team with transportation and snacks.

Awards Along the Journey

Along this journey, Cadettes have the opportunity to earn three prestigious leadership awards that engage them in improving the world's air quality while also supporting and nourishing their own abilities as leaders who are aware, alert, and able to affirm all they do.

In the girls' book, activities leading to the awards are marked by the icon on the right. Here are the three awards and the steps Cadettes take to earn them:

1 Keep an Air Log throughout the journey. Record what you see, hear, feel, and smell in the air.

2 Identify two experts who can guide you to greater air awareness (meteorologists, biologists, wind farm or aeronautical engineers, parasailing instructors, astronauts, physicians or other health specialists, fragrance specialists, yoga instructors.)

3 Increase your AWAREness about the issues that impact Earth's air. Check out all the air issues throughout *Breathe*. Take a walk, with some Cadette friends (and of course a trusty adult), around a school, business district, a mall, or other area in search of air issues. Think about trees (see pages 52–63 in the girls' book) or think about noise (see pages 17–31 in the girls' book)!

4 Decide the most important, personal reason you care about Earth's air. Write a statement that explains why this reason matters to you and why it should matter to others. Share your AWAREness statement with your sister Cadettes.

1 With your Cadette team, choose an air issue to act on together. Learn as much as you can about it (use experts you've met) and write a statement that explains why it's important to educate and inspire others on this issue.

2 Decide whom to educate and inspire—this is your Air Care Team (ACT)! What groups of people would be best to join with you? Principals and teachers? Parents? Your peers? Who can best assist you in moving forward?

3 Decide what you will ask your Air Care Team to do. What call to action will you deliver as you educate and inspire? How will your ACT's efforts on this call to action improve your air issue?

4 Decide how to reach your Air Care Team to inspire them to act on your air issue. The medium and method are up to you. The goal is to engage all their senses and create a sustainable effort! Air needs more than just a one-time gathering!

5 Educate and inspire! Give your ACT its call to action. Feel the rewards of influencing others in a lasting way!

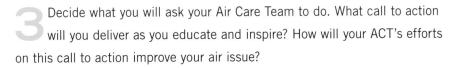

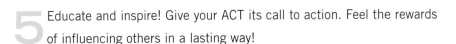

1 Gather proof of progress or improvement through your efforts to educate and inspire. What is the ACT doing to benefit air?

2 Share the impact with your ACT and maybe even go further. Contact a local media outlet or ask your library for display space.

3 Get with your Cadette team and reflect on your efforts and their impact. Take some time and talk it through. What will you do differently the next time you decide to act for Earth?

4 Affirm your commitment to strive to be an heir apparent of air and all of Planet Earth's elements.

Health, Safety, and Well-Being

Girl Scouting is guided by a positive philosophy of inclusion that benefits all. On this journey, it is hoped that girls will increase their feelings of being powerful, capable, and strong as they enhance their skills and develop new ones. So, as the Girl Scout Law says, "be a sister to every Girl Scout." Be sensitive to whether any girls are new to town, have a disability, don't speak English as a first language, or have parents getting a divorce. Often what counts most is being open-minded and aware, staying flexible, and creatively varying your approach with the girls.

The emotional and physical safety and well-being of girls is of paramount importance in Girl Scouting. Look out for the safety of girls by keeping *Volunteer Essentials* and the Girl Scout reference "Safety Activity Checkpoints" handy. And when planning all gatherings and trips, be sure to:

- Check into any additional safety guidelines your Girl Scout council might provide, based on local issues.
- Talk to girls and their families about special needs or concerns.

Welcoming Girls with Disabilities

First, don't assume that because a person has a disability, she needs assistance or special accommodations. Probably the most important thing you can do is to ask the individual girl or her parents or guardians what she needs to make her experience in Girl Scouts successful. If you are frank and accessible to the girl and her parents, it's likely they will respond in kind, creating a better experience for all.

It's important for all girls to be rewarded based on their best efforts—not completion of a task. Give any girl the opportunity to do her best and she will. Sometimes that means changing a few rules or approaching an activity in a more creative way. Here are a few examples:

- Invite a girl to perform an activity after observing others doing it first.
- Ask the girls to come up with ideas for how to adapt an activity.

Often what counts most is staying flexible and varying your approach.

For a list of online resources, visit www.girlscouts.org and search on "disability resources."

Snacks

Food is a great way to bring people together—and, of course, it offers an energy boost. Talk to girls about their snack plans for gatherings. Check in about food allergies, too!

You and the Cadettes might experiment with snack treats that are airy and uplifting: whipped yogurt cheese on wheat crackers, herbal iced tea, carrots with yogurt dip. For a special treat, the Cadettes might try one of the airy dessert recipes in their book (see pages 50–51 and 88–89).

GIRL SCOUT COUNCIL CONTACT INFO

Name:_____

_____

_____

Can help with:_____

_____

_____

Phone:_____

E-mail:_____

Breezing into Math, Science, and Engineering

Walks along the beach enjoying fresh ocean air, hikes up a mountain trail, pauses to watch hawks or eagles soar—all of these Cadette-worthy activities engage girls in understanding the scientific fact that life on Earth depends on air. People, animals, plants, microscopic organisms—everything alive needs air.

As the Cadettes learn about the air all around them, they will see that science, math, and engineering are as much a part of daily life as the air they breathe. Yet a troublesome gap often develops between girls' interest and ability in these subjects and their desire and confidence to pursue higher education, and ultimately careers, in these fields. By eighth grade, only half as many girls as boys in the United States are interested in careers in science, technology, engineering, and math (STEM). Those numbers get even worse in high school and college. Fewer than 1 in 5 of all college engineering degrees are awarded to women. And even among these women, a great many leave the profession in their 30s and 40s. Women are also under-represented in the fields of chemistry and physics.

BUILDING SCIENTIFIC MINDS

To sustain interest and build confidence, Girl Scouts believes that early exposure to the joys and wonders of these subjects is crucial—as is encouragement from families, teachers, and the media that is so much a part of daily life. What's key is ending the many myths and biases that girls encounter when pursuing these subjects. The other part of the challenge is for girls to realize that science, technology, engineering, and math offer ways to help people and communities. On this journey, Cadettes have a direct opportunity to experience how essential these subjects are to any desire to protect Planet Earth. *Breathe* aims to foster lifelong interests in these subjects, and in every aspect of air.

So take advantage of each time STEM subjects pop up in the girls' lives. Sirens in the night? A lesson in decibels. Cell phones beeping? Modern technology as daily distraction. A line of smog or a fresh ocean breeze? A reminder of Earth's atmosphere, and how countries halfway around the world are our next-door neighbors when it comes to air.

As *Breathe* makes clear, even kitchen chemistry involves endless airy transformations. Making bread or baking cakes combines chemistry and a lot of math—ratios, measurements, proportions. What's a measuring cup, after all, but a basic math tool? A flattened cake pulled from the oven might signal a scientific misfire. Not enough eggs, perhaps? Or no baking powder? And think of souffles, cream puffs, and popovers and all their exacting needs. Cooks might dispense with measuring tools, but bakers rarely can. Even the most intuitive of them play by the numbers.

Make the most of every creative scientific moment that arises. If you and the girls try your hand at fashioning kites from plastic bags for a group of Brownies, be attuned to the air when you set them in flight. If the wind takes hold and your kites soar, that's one more airy pleasure to celebrate, one more way to see that atmospheric science is part of each and every day. Take a deep breath and prepare to enjoy some soaring moments with the girls.

WOMEN IN SPACE

On Oct. 25, 2007, some 200 miles above Earth, the Space Shuttle *Discovery* docked with the International Space Station, the hatches between the ships opened, and the two commanders followed standard NASA etiquette: They shook hands. But this handshake was one for the history books. The commanders of both missions were women: Pam Melroy and Peggy Whitson.

"It was no publicity stunt," says shuttle commander Melroy. Enough women had worked their way into leadership positions at NASA that a handshake like this was now possible.

Many more women work on the ground at NASA. Melroy recalls the women working on just one mission being called together for a photo. "Everyone was amazed and inspired when they realized the room was filled to nearly bursting!" she says.

"The first woman to walk on Mars is in school today. Let's not let her down—let's help her get there."

—Pam Melroy, commander, Space Shuttle *Discovery*

15

Cadettes and the Great Outdoors

Cadettes like to do it all. Hiking, camping, canoeing. So get out with the girls as much as you can to enjoy air in a way that engages all their senses. Take walks, have picnics, explore a nature preserve or a park. Any outdoor adventure offers an opportunity to enjoy fresh sights and scents, and the sounds and silent spaces of nature.

Each time you venture out, encourage the girls to search out their own quiet spaces, away from the beeps and twitters of electronic gadgets. The Cadettes may be inspired by the One Square Inch of Silence project (see page 23 of the girls' book). Just as noise in one small area spreads out and affects the larger landscape, silence has the same effect. One Square Inch of Silence has the power to keep the silence going all around it! Guide the girls to find their own silent space, and perhaps even mark it with a special ceremony.

Harvesting Wind Field Trip

As wind farms spring up all over the country, trips to these new fields for harvesting clean, sustainable energy are easier to plan. Check out the information on pages 91–97 of the girls' book.

Wind farms range from family windmill generators to vast acres of sleek, slowly turning wind turbines powering municipalities and regions. Larger wind farms have community relations departments that will welcome your group and offer planning tools before the visit.

A visit to a wind farm will make a good springboard for discussions about:

- the new "green economy" versus the old "pollution-based economy" that relies on fossil fuels
- "green collar" jobs that cut fossil fuel emissions, curb global warming, and offer exciting new career possibilities and good paychecks
- wind power and solar power as renewable energy technologies that tap into natural cycles and systems
- sustainability—a word that describes renewable forms of energy, the girls' project, their commitment, and perhaps the girls' future careers.

Girl Scout Traditions and Ceremonies

Even the briefest of ceremonies can take girls away from the everyday to think about hopes, intentions, commitments, and feelings. A ceremony marks a separation from whatever girls have just come from (school, work, dance class, math club) and creates the sense that what will happen now is special and important. So find out how and when girls want ceremonies.

Ceremonies can be as simple as gathering in a friendship circle, lighting a candle, and saying to oneself—or sharing—one hope or affirmation, or reflecting together on one line of the Girl Scout Law. Or girls might read poems, play music, or sing songs. Invite them to create their own simple ways to mark their time together as special. You'll also find various suggestions in the Sample Sessions.

QUIET SIGN

The Quiet Sign is a way to silence a crowd without shouting at anyone. The sign is made by holding up the right hand with all five fingers extended. It refers to the original Fifth Law of Girl Scouting: A Girl Scout is courteous.

SWAPS

Trading SWAPS (Special Whatchamacallits Affectionately Pinned Somewhere) is a beloved Girl Scout tradition of exchanging small keepsakes. It started long ago when Girl Scouts and Girl Guides from England first gathered for fun, song, and making new friends. SWAPS are still a fun way for Girl Scouts to meet and promote friendship. Each SWAP offers a memory of a special event or a particular girl. A SWAP usually says something about a Girl Scout's group or highlights something special about where she lives. And it's simple—it could be made from donated or recycled goods. What airy SWAPS will Cadettes think of? Maybe they can network with other Cadettes in the region on the *Breathe* journey and, well, swap airy souvenirs!

Earning the LiA

Girl Scouts has always had a tradition of older girls helping younger girls. In the *It's Your Planet—Love It* series of leadership journeys, Cadettes have air and Brownies have water. Think of the power of bringing these two grade levels and all their Girl Scout power together! That's what the LiA (Leader in Action) Award is all about.

The LiA encourages Cadettes to be key assistants on a Brownie team's *WOW! Wonders of Water* journey. All the steps to the award are in the Cadette LiA letter on pages 20–21 of this guide and also online in the journey section of girlscouts.org. Just photocopy them and encourage Cadettes to go for the award.

Since many Cadettes will be journeying through *Breathe*, you might network with the Girl Scout community in your region. How great it would be if a pair of Cadettes could assist a group of Brownies whose backgrounds and experience—geographic, cultural, ethnic, religious, physical, or otherwise—vary from their own. The Cadettes and the younger girls could learn from one another, and also reach toward an important Girl Scout leadership outcome: Girls advance diversity in a multicultural world.

Ask your council for assistance in linking up with other Girl Scout groups.

Dear Girl Scout Cadette,

Just as you are *Breathe*-ing your way through a journey about air—your own and everyone else's, you've got some (actually around 800,000) little sisters who are on a journey about water—theirs—and everyone else's!

You've got air and the Brownies have water! And, of course, both are essential to life—and both are quite wondrous and awe-inspiring when you stop and appreciate them!

So, earn yourself the LiA (Leader in Action) badge by sharing some of your savvy for Earth (not to mention all of your other flairs) with a team of Brownies in your community.

Here's how:

1. **Identify a team of Girl Scout Brownies** on (or about to be on) their *WOW! Wonders of Water* journey. Or find a team that recently completed *WOW!* Ask your Girl Scout council for tips on how to locate a Brownie team.

2. **Talk to the volunteer guiding the Brownies** and find out what the team is doing, what the Brownies enjoy, and what the volunteer finds challenging. Take a look at the Brownie *WOW!* book and flip through the adult book, too!

Now the fun begins!

3. **Arrange to be at some of the Brownie Team's gatherings,** coordinating the schedule with the volunteers so you'll have time to do each of these:

☐ Guide the Brownies through a fun activity that teaches them something about Earth's air or water or both! You can adapt an activity from your journey for younger girls, check out some of the options in the *WOW!* girls' book and volunteer books, or create an activity of your own. A magical science experiment? Making rainbows? Making and flying a kite? Enjoy the sounds of nature? Scenty stuff? A game you invent about animals that inhabit water and sky? Or perhaps you and some friends can act out a scene from "A Very Wet ELF Adventure" or even make a short puppet show based on the story. Better yet, guide the Brownies to do their own!
Date accomplished _____

☐ Inspire the Brownies to try a new healthy habit—a watery treat (check out the ideas in the *WOW!* book), some fun cardio or yoga exercises, or a fruit or veggie grown with local water (and air!). Check with the Brownie's volunteer about food allergies before you plan any snacks. Your goal is to get the Brownies thinking about how what is good for us is often good for Earth, too! Date accomplished _____

☐ Engage the Brownies in a short activity that gets them thinking about what great teamwork looks like. Maybe you know a game or maybe you can invent one that gets the Brownies cooperating. If not, get some ideas from other Girl Scouts in your area. Teach the game as an opening or closing or an energizing break. While the Brownies are exploring the Wonders of Water, they are also practicing another WOW—Ways of Working. Your goal is to get the Brownies practicing some really great WOWs! Date accomplished _____

☐ Share with the Brownies a line from the Girl Scout Law that you are trying to live out in your life right now. Tell them what you are doing to bring that line to life. Then, ask them to tell you about a line they are living out! Date accomplished _____

4. **After you've completed your mission with the Brownies,** ask the volunteer for input on what you did. What was great? What might you want to do a little differently in the future?

5. **Now that you've enjoyed some time inspiring Brownies,** think about and answer these questions:

- What did you **Discover** within yourself as you guided Brownies?

- Why it is important to **Connect** with younger girls?

- What did you accomplish on behalf of the Earth by **Taking Action** to educate and inspire Brownies?

CONGRATULATIONS! Wear your LiA with pride!

What + How: Creating a Quality Experience

It's not just "what" girls do, but "how" they are engaged that creates a high-quality Girl Scout experience. All Girl Scout experiences are built on three processes that make Girl Scouting unique from school and other extracurricular activities. When used together, these processes—Girl Led, Learning by Doing, and Cooperative Learning—ensure the quality and promote the fun and friendship so integral to Girl Scouting. Take some time to understand these processes and how to use them with Cadettes.

Girl Led

"Girl Led" is just what it sounds like—girls play an active part in figuring out the what, where, when, how, and why of their activities. So coach the girls to lead the planning, decision-making, learning, and fun as much as possible. This ensures that girls are engaged in their learning and experience leadership opportunities as they prepare to become active participants in their local and global communities. With Cadettes, you could:

- encourage girls to plan challenging activities or tasks and serve as a resource for them

- promote discussion and debate, giving guidelines for depersonalizing arguments—debate without "finger-pointing"

- expose girls to opportunities to teach or guide others, and support girls in providing service to and for others

Learning by Doing

Learning by Doing is a hands-on learning process that engages girls in continuous cycles of action and reflection that result in deeper understanding of concepts and mastery of practical skills. As they participate in meaningful activities and then reflect on them, girls get to explore their own questions, discover answers, gain new skills, and share ideas and observations with others. Throughout the process, it's important for girls to be able to connect their experiences to their lives and apply what they have learned to their future experiences both within and outside of Girl Scouting. With Cadettes, you could:

KEEP IT GIRL LED

Remember: You want the girls to take a major role in planning and executing this leadership experience. They may first want you to come up with the ideas and plans. *But hold your ground!* This is the girls' experience, and they're up to the challenge.

From beginning to end, keep your eye on what the girls want to do and the direction they seem to be taking. It's the approach begun by Juliette Gordon Low: When she and her associates couldn't decide on a new direction, she often said, "Let's ask the girls!" At each session, ask the girls for any last thoughts on what they've done or discussed.

- ask critical questions to challenge girls to think more deeply or engage more fully in a learning experience

- enable girls to experiment with ways to solve real-life problems and to share their methods with others

- ask girls what would be the best way to teach something to other people, and then help them work out a graphic or demo

Cooperative Learning

Through cooperative learning, girls work together toward shared goals in an atmosphere of respect and collaboration that encourages the sharing of skills, knowledge, and learning. Moreover, given that many girls desire to connect with others, cooperative learning may be a particularly meaningful and enjoyable way to engage girls in learning. Working together in all-girl environments also encourages girls to feel powerful and emotionally and physically safe, and it allows them to experience a sense of belonging even in the most diverse groups.

With Cadettes, you could:

- encourage girls to plan and participate in challenging activities or tasks that involve the entire group in decision-making and carrying out activities

- observe cooperative learning groups, but act only as a resource for girls so that girls do most of the planning

- support girls' learning effective communication skills around conflict resolution within the group

LEARNING BY DOING

The girls have many opportunities to reflect on their journey experiences and apply them to their lives throughout *Breathe*. Check out the "Heir Apparent" exercise suggested in this guide (pages 92–93) for the journey's closing celebration. This gives girls a way to reflect on everything they have learned on the journey.

FLAIR FOR TEAMWORK

Throughout the journey the girls take part activities that build teamwork and cooperation. Starting in Session 1, the Cadettes have some fun with a team effort to raise the blare in the air. Throughout the journey, you might ask each girl to reflect on how her teammates' thoughts and actions have expanded her view of the world.

Seeing Processes and Outcomes Play Out in *Breathe*

Girl Scout processes and leadership outcomes play out in a variety of ways during team gatherings, but often they are so seamless you might not notice them. For example, in Session 4 (pages 60–61), the Cadettes take part in an air-quality Observational Field Trip that sets the stage for their ALERT project. The call-outs below show how the Girl Scout processes make the ceremony at the close of this activity a learning and growing experience for girls—and up the fun, too! Throughout *Breathe*, you'll see processes and outcomes play out again and again. Before you know it, you'll be using these valuable aspects of Girl Scouting in whatever Cadettes do—from going for the Girl Scout Silver Award to taking a trip to Girl Scout Cookie Activities!

This is a nice transition out of the cycle of action and reflection in the **Learning by Doing** process and right into **Girl Led**. As the girls reflect on their air observations— perhaps through the writing of the personal statement itself—they get to know themselves and their values a little better. This progression is building toward a combination of the Cadette-level **Discover outcomes Girls develop a strong sense of self** and **Girls develop positive values**. And as girls gain expertise in their own feelings and beliefs, they are able to express what they've learned for the benefit of themselves and the group. This expression is **Girl Led**.

FROM SAMPLE SESSION 4

GET AWARE

Closing Ceremony

Let the team know that they have made excellent progress toward earning their AWARE awards—and perhaps even completed all the steps! Encourage the team to check out the steps on the Award Tracker on page 102–103 of their book. What do they have left to do? If they have not yet talked to some experts, what ideas do they have about doing so?

Note that the last step to earning AWARE is for each girl to write a personal statement about why she cares about air, one that she will share with the rest of the team. The girls can do this now, as their closing, or opt to do so at the opening of their next gathering.

If they need a little assistance to get going, ask a few questions, like these:

- *What have you become more aware of related to air in our lives since* Breathe *started?*

These questions help girls learn more about their values and beliefs regarding air quality, and they are also specifically about people's health. This ties to the **Discover outcome Girls gain practical life skills—girls practice healthy living**. At the Cadette grade level, the girls' reflection upon this issue shows their commitment to promoting healthy behavior.

- *What matters to you: Making more quiet time to tune into ourselves and nature? Dealing with the source of smells that are bad for us to breathe in? Trying to prevent kids from smoking? Making sure we have more plants and trees?*

- *Why do these things matter to you? Why be AWARE and care?*

- *Isn't it interesting how what is good for Earth is good for us, too?*

Consider also using the closing today to engage girls in thinking about all the interesting education and career possibilities available to them. There are so many to gain AWAREness of!

Suggest they flip through their book for a few minutes and select their favorite from among the women and girls doing something for Earth. Then, ask the girls to say a few words about what new possibilities the story makes them AWARE of and why they are intrigued. You can do this as a large group or in small teams.

In addition to thinking about the women featured in their book, girls could also think about what they have learned from any guests they have networked with during *Breathe* gatherings, or stories they are AWARE of in the news.

This is the **Cooperative Learning** process. Girls team up, either in small groups or one large one, to share their thoughts and ideas on their new awareness of environmental careers.

Ceremonies should be **Girl Led**. Though the volunteer suggests that girls flip through their book, it is the girl who decides which woman most appeals to her.

The reading and thinking the girls are asked to do here opens them up to a range of women doing good for the planet. In their choice of a favorite female leader, they must first assess (consciously or unconsciously) their own values. This moves them toward the **Discover outcome Girls develop positive values.**

This activity also relates to the **Connect outcome Girls feel connected to their community, locally and globally.** The women and girls featured in their book give the Cadettes a sense of belonging to a community of women and girls working in support of the environment.

Understanding the Journey's Leadership Benefits

Filled with fun and friendship, *Breathe* is designed to develop the skills and values girls need to be leaders now and as they grow. *Breathe* activities are designed to enable Cadettes to progress toward achieving 10 of 15 national outcomes, or benefits, of the Girl Scout Leadership Experience, as summarized on the next page.

Each girl is different, so don't expect them all to exhibit the same signs to indicate what they are learning along the journey. What matters is that you are guiding the Cadettes toward leadership skills and qualities they can use right now—and all their lives.

For full definitions of the outcomes and the signs that Girl Scout Cadettes are achieving them, see *Transforming Leadership: Focusing on Outcomes of the New Girl Scout Leadership Experience* (GSUSA, 2008). Keep in mind that the intended benefits to girls are the cumulative result of traveling through an entire journey—and everything else girls experience in Girl Scouting.

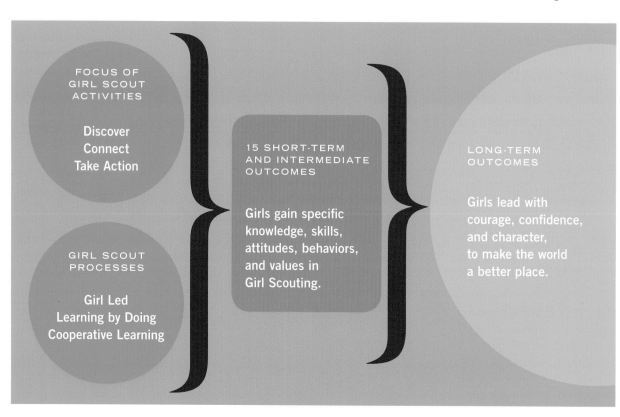

FOCUS OF
GIRL SCOUT
ACTIVITIES

Discover
Connect
Take Action

GIRL SCOUT
PROCESSES

Girl Led
Learning by Doing
Cooperative Learning

15 SHORT-TERM
AND INTERMEDIATE
OUTCOMES

Girls gain specific
knowledge, skills,
attitudes, behaviors,
and values in
Girl Scouting.

LONG-TERM
OUTCOMES

Girls lead with
courage, confidence,
and character,
to make the world
a better place.

NATIONAL LEADERSHIP OUTCOMES

	AT THE CADETTE LEVEL, girls...	RELATED ACTIVITIES (by Session number or girls' book page)	SAMPLE "SIGN" when the outcome is achieved, girls might...
DISCOVER — Girls develop a strong sense of self.	show an increase in self-efficacy.	GB: Flair, p. 49	report increased belief in their ability to achieve personal goals.
Girls develop positive values.	are better able to examine their own and others' values from individual, cultural, and global perspectives.	GB: Profiles of women and girls; Aware Award, p. 104–105	report greater appreciation for the diversity of values based on individual and/or cultural differences.
Girls gain practical life skills—girls practice healthy living.	are increasingly committed to practicing and promoting healthy behavior.	S2: Scent Sense; S3: Relaxed; GB: Music to Your Ears? Noise, Noise Level, pp. 20–25; Need Some Space, p. 27 and 77; Elevate Your Air Power, p. 75	report increased interest in learning more about how exercise, diet, relaxation, and other activities can give balance to their lives.
Girls develop healthy relationships.	are able to use positive communication and relationship-building skills.	GB: Air It Out, p. 30.	give examples of behaviors they use to promote mutual respect, trust, and understanding.
CONNECT — Girls promote cooperation and team building.	have a greater understanding of team building.	S6: Adding Our Flair; S7: Team Check	list criteria for what makes a good team (e.g., clear roles, trust, respect, diversity).
Girls promote cooperation and team building.	are better able to address obstacles to effective group work and team building.	S8: Pulse Check Teamwork	describe obstacles to group work (e.g., not being willing to compromise, concern with individual interests over group goals, always wanting to be the person talking) and suggest possible solutions.
Girls feel connected to their communities, locally and globally.	strengthen existing relationships and seek to create new connections with others in their communities.	S6: Sounding the Call; GB: Alert, pp. 106–108	feel more confident contacting community members for help with community service and action projects (e.g., teachers, youth organizations, after-school clubs).
TAKE ACTION — Girls can identify community needs.	strengthen their ability to decide which community issue deserves action.	S4: Get Aware Observational Trip; S5: Observing the Observations; GB: Compare Air log, pp. 14–15; No Idling Zone, pp. 44–45; Get out in the Air and Permanent Paper Reduction, p. 63; What's in Your Air?, p. 67	report using a variety of tools (e.g., community mapping, interviewing, observations) to identify needs, assets, and potential impact of their planned projects.
Girls are resourceful problem solvers.	are able to create and implement detailed action plans for their projects.	S3: Planning for Air Care Field Observation; S5: Choosing an Alert; S7: Planning and Conducting a Meeting	demonstrate independence in thinking through required components of their action plans (e.g., location of resources, time lines, responsibilities).
Girls are resourceful problem solvers.	increasingly seek out community support and resources to help achieve their goals.	S6: Identifying the Air Care Team; S7 and S8: ALERT Award	identify people/organizations in their communities to help on some aspect of their project.
Girls advocate for themselves and others, locally and globally.	recognize the importance of advocacy in accomplishing positive changes for themselves and others.	S8: Gathering Some Affirmations	give examples of how youth can influence and/or participate in community decision-making (e.g., influence the library to remain open longer, start a teen hotline, form an antidiscrimination group).
Girls educate and inspire others to act.	show increased commitment to educate others on how to better their communities.	S9: Opening Ceremony: Affirm	organize a show-and-tell for younger Girl Scouts to educate them about how to be more active in community affairs.

S=Session, GB=Girls' Book

From *aMAZE* to *Breathe*

If your Cadette team has already enjoyed the *aMAZE*, keep those experiences growing by linking some of its "key" leadership ideas to the *Breathe* journey. You might talk to the girls about how their *aMAZE* experiences engaged them in positive relationship strategies that they can put to use in *Breathe*. For example:

- When the team needs to straighten out disagreements or deal with hurt feelings, "I-Statements" will come in handy.

- Perhaps the girls have relationship techniques in their *aMAZE* Peace Kits that will help them reach out and build an Air Care Team.

As the Cadettes travel through *Breathe*, take a moment from time to time to get them talking about these key communication strategies. For example, you might ask:

- *What have you noticed about adjusting your communication style depending on whom you are talking to?*

- *When we team up on our ALERT project, what communication strategies are we using the most?*

- *How are our connections growing through these strategies?*

- *When we act to save Earth, how do our communication styles help us as leaders?*

If the Cadettes enjoyed the various team-building activities or ceremonies of *aMAZE*, by all means continue them in *Breathe*, too!

Your Perspective on Leadership

The Girl Scout Leadership philosophy—Discover + Connect + Take Action—implies that leadership happens from the inside out. Your thoughts, enthusiasm, and approach will influence the Cadettes, so take some time to reflect on your own perspective on leadership. Take a few minutes now—and throughout *Breathe*—to apply the three "keys" of leadership to yourself. You may find it useful to network with fellow volunteers and share ideas about your progress as you guide girls through this journey!

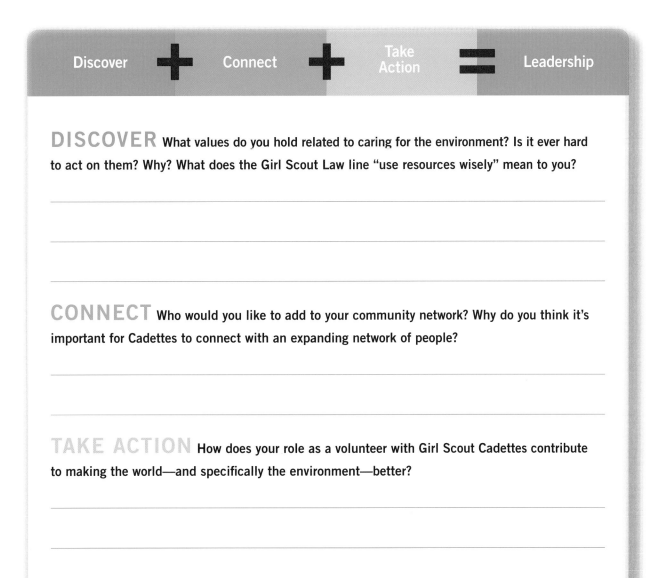

Discover ➕ **Connect** ➕ **Take Action** ➡️ **Leadership**

DISCOVER What values do you hold related to caring for the environment? Is it ever hard to act on them? Why? What does the Girl Scout Law line "use resources wisely" mean to you?

CONNECT Who would you like to add to your community network? Why do you think it's important for Cadettes to connect with an expanding network of people?

TAKE ACTION How does your role as a volunteer with Girl Scout Cadettes contribute to making the world—and specifically the environment—better?

"First, there is the power of the Wind, constantly exerted over the globe . . . Here is an almost incalculable power at our disposal, yet how trifling the use we make of it!"

— Henry David Thoreau, "Paradise (to be) Regained,"1834

The Journey's 10 Sample Sessions

This guide offers a sample schedule of 10 sessions, each lasting about 90 minutes. You may find that each sample session provides more activities and examples than you and the girls can or will want to cover. Let the length and content of your gatherings be determined by the girls' interests, your own, and such matters as how much time the girls have to spend on the journey.

From the first session, you may want to encourage the girls to keep their own air space in mind. How is it? What does it need? What might improve it?

Ahead of each gathering with the Cadettes, you'll find it useful to read through the sample session, or the revised session you have developed in partnership with the girls. Thinking about the session as a whole lets you concentrate on the potential impact of each discussion and activity. At the start of sessions, you'll see handy Prepare Ahead tips. Some involve material preparations; others relate to session topics and offer ideas about how to approach them with the girls. Following these tips will ensure that you're ready to guide girls forward in a fresh and enjoyable way.

What You'll Find in Each Session

KEEP BASIC MATERIALS HANDY

A box or bag with markers, pens, scrap paper, glue, scissors, and masking tape will prove handy to bring to the sessions. Perhaps girls and their families can help round up these basic supplies—leftovers will do. If your meeting space has a chalkboard or newsprint and easel you can use, that's great. Otherwise, you might want to have a few poster boards or sheets of newsprint handy. Don't invest in anything expensive—recycle file folders, use the back of posters, and so on. A few sessions also note other simple materials specific to the suggested activities.

AT A GLANCE: The session's goal, activities, and a list of simple materials you'll need.

What to Say: Examples of what to say and ask the Cadettes along *Breathe* as you link activities, reflections, and learning experiences. Must you read from the "script"? Absolutely not! The girls (and you) will have far more fun if you take the main ideas from the examples provided and then just be yourself.

Activity Instructions: Tips for guiding the girls through activities and experiences along *Breathe*, and plenty of "tools" (charts, suggestions for reflections, etc.) to correspond to the experiences on the journey.

Coaching to Create a Quality Experience: The quality of the Girl Scout Leadership Experience depends greatly on three processes—Girl Led, Learning by Doing, and Cooperative Learning. By following the prompts in this guide for activities, reflections, girl choice-making, and discussions, you'll be using the processes—with ease.

Tying Activities to Impact: This guide notes the purpose of the journey's activities and discussions, so you'll always understand the intended benefit to girls. You'll even be able to see the benefits—by observing the "signs" that the girls are achieving the national Girl Scout Leadership Outcomes.

Customizing the Journey

Think of these sample sessions as the main route through *Breathe*—they will get you and the girls from each step to the next, accomplishing goals along the way. As on any journey, if you and your passengers have the time, use your imagination to venture off the main route now and then to take some real-life deep breaths and meet some sister environmental travelers. Consider, for example:

Fresh Perspectives

Hearing about the experiences of older girls and women can add fresh perspectives to the knowledge Cadettes gain through *Breathe.* You don't need to look very far to expand the horizons of middle schoolers. They respect high school girls, so you might invite Girl Scout Seniors and Ambassadors, or other teen community members, to present their own insights on the journey's topics (it's also a chance for the older teens to develop their leadership skills).

Creative Stuff

Girls who like to make things—crafts, foods, DIY (Do It Yourself) projects, inventions, videos—will enjoy sharing their talents with the team. So encourage the girls to share their "favorite to-do's" with each other. They might surprise one another with gifts they make, which puts a breathtaking twist on their creativity!

RETREATS

A weekend away from it all (maybe even at a Girl Scout camp) is a great way for girls to engage in the discussions and role-playing that await them in *Breathe.*

MAKING MEMORIES

If the Cadettes want to create a visual record of any activity along the journey, encourage them to bring to the sessions cameras, video cameras, or cell phones with photo/video capability.

Two Great Ways to Share the Air! Have a sleepover on air mattresses or a sleep-out under the stars.

SAMPLE SESSION 1
Blare in the Air!

AT A GLANCE

Goal: Cadettes explore the noises people routinely send through the air, and then experience the sound of silence as a team. They begin to think about the Earth sounds they love and how what they value can influence how they choose to care for Earth's air.

- Symphony of Noise: The Journey Begins

- Above the Noise: Team Challenges

- Weighing in on Noise and Silence

- Imagining the Sounds of Earth

- Journey Logistics

- Closing Ceremony: Tuning In

MATERIALS

- **Symphony of Noise:** noise-making gadgets, including those that girls may routinely carry (cell phones, portable music players, etc.). Try to round up a portable stereo or boom box, a mini TV and DVD player (or a computer with speakers), and some simple instruments (kazoos, party horns, etc.)

- **Above the Noise:** challenge slips (page 37); a timer, clock, or watch

- **Imagining the Sounds of Earth:** a few postcards or a photo or two from magazines or books to help the girls think about the natural sounds Earth makes;

PREPARE AHEAD

- Chat with any assistants about their roles before and during the session.

- Read through this session, plus the introduction and "The Sound of Silence" section in the girls' book (starting on page 17).

- Consider sound in your own life: Think about the noise in your air—noises you enjoy, noises that make you feel frazzled, the times that you have enjoyed silence, and the times that you have enjoyed nature's noises. What do you love about Earth's silences and sounds? How might this shape your values related to caring for Earth's air? Set up the Symphony of Noise.

AS GIRLS ARRIVE

Explain the "Symphony of Noise" to a Cadette or two who arrive early and invite them to lead it. Ask them to set up all the noisemaking devices in a big cluster in the middle of the room. To get some background noise going, turn a TV on and put in a DVD, or have a radio on hand.

Jot down "Above the Noise" challenges (page 37) on slips of paper and place them in a jar or bag. Then put the jar where everyone can reach it.

ON THE LOOKOUT FOR AIR EXPERTS

Throughout the journey, you may hear of a family friend or relative who is in a profession related to the air topics at hand. Jot the name down and encourage the girls to think of such people as potential experts worth talking to and learning from.

Symphony of Noise: The Journey Begins

Invite the girls to gather in a circle around the noisemakers. Encourage them to add to the noisemakers by taking out their cell phones, music players, or anything else they have that might add to the din.

Introduce the activity by saying: *We're going to use our gadgets at the same time to send as much noise into the air as we can. On the count of three, everybody ring, blast, call, use your speakerphone, set off alarms, or do anything else you can think of to make noise. Let it all buzz, ping, ring, sing, ding. And groove along if you want to!*

Round 1: Invite a girl to volunteer to be the "conductor." Explain that she'll start the "orchestra" on the count of three and then, after a few minutes of noise, hold up her hand (the Girl Scout Quiet Sign). Tell the group that is the signal for everyone to turn off the noisemakers, hold up their hands, and become silent.

Round 1 continues for a few minutes. Then allow silence to settle over the group for a minute or two.

Ask a few questions about what is enjoyable and what is challenging related to all the noise and noisemaking gadgets we have in our lives:

- What does it feel like to make a lot of noise?
- What do you love about your phone, music player, etc.?
- When is enough enough?

Round 2: Guide the group into Round 2 by saying: *OK, we are going to do it again, but this time we are going to add a little challenge that symbolizes the challenges we often face—concentrating on getting something done and communicating with one another amid all the noise and distractions in our world.*

So, again, make all the noise you can, while you also take turns choosing an "Above the Noise" challenge slip from the jar. You will each try to lead the team in the challenge.

After the first person goes, continue around the circle, taking turns leading one another to accomplish the task on your slip. Just keep it moving. Silly is OK! And don't forget: Make all the noise you can while you multitask on the challenge.

After we've each had a turn, or there are no more slips, the last person to lead gives the Quiet Sign and sets the timer for five minutes. We will try sitting in silence together for those five minutes! Everybody ready?

ABOVE THE NOISE: TEAM CHALLENGES

Jot these challenges, and any others that you can think of, on slips of paper. The challenges can be any "silly little thing" that engages the team in doing something together amid all the noise. Ask girls to add their own!

- *Everyone, answer together: What is 8 x 9?*
- *Shout your birthday (go one by one around the circle)*
- *All together now: Recite the alphabet*
- *Spell out "noise" together*
- *Do 10 jumping jacks, all together*
- *Take a deep breath and then exhale*
- *Everyone, shout a word that rhymes with "air"—no repeats!*
- *Do a crazy dance move together*
- *Send a wave around the circle*
- *All together now: Count backward from 15*

When everyone has had a chance to lead, remind the last girl to signal the group into silence, using the Girl Scout Quiet Sign, and start the timer. Don't worry if there is giggling or fidgeting during the five minutes—just keep at it.

Weighing in on Noise and Silence

Now that the team has experienced both a big blare and silence, start a conversation about the noise in our lives and the value of silence. If the girls are struggling a little, it's a good time to share some of your own examples or anecdotes. Here are some guiding questions:

- *What's good about our noisemaking gadgets?*
- *Do you like to stay plugged into your music even when you're with others? If so, why?*
- *Do you ever put in your earbuds to signal that you want to be alone? When do you take out your earbuds? What's it like when you are with other people who are wearing earbuds?*
- *Can you think of times and examples when noise gets in our way of really connecting with others? With enjoying things? With concentrating?*
- *Do you ever wish you were a little less connected and available when someone needs to reach you? Or maybe that you had a little less information at your fingertips? When and why? What about other kinds of noise that distract us? Advertising? Traffic? Anything else?*

TIPS FOR SHARING AND DISCUSSING

For discussions or activities in large groups, you might want to split into smaller teams and give each one a question or two, then have teams report back to the whole group when you gather together again.

- *What was it like to sit in silence together? (If there was giggling or fidgeting, let the girls know that's normal because most people are not used to being silent together.)*

- *Does five minutes of silence feel like a little or a lot?*

- *What ideas do you have about how silent time together can contribute to our strength as individuals? As a team?*

- *Do any of you enjoy silence in other ways, such as yoga or meditation? What do you gain from it?*

Imagining the Sounds of Earth

Transition the girls to thinking about the sounds of nature. Give them a blank piece of paper (or perhaps they'd like to write in their *Breathe* books) and say: *Imagine Earth with no people noises. What do you hear and how does it make you feel? Take a few minutes and capture your feelings in words or with a sentence or a doodle. Think of your favorite memory of being in nature (for example, a snowy day or a quiet morning on a beach). What do you hear?*

Have on hand a few postcards or a photo or two from magazines or books to help the girls think about the natural sounds Earth makes.

Invite the girls to share their favorite Earth sounds and how the sounds make them feel.

Move into a discussion about how our daily noises sometimes get in the way of taking the time to appreciate and care for the planet. You might say something like: *We hear so much about how we as a society are depleting Earth's resources and about all the environmental problems that must be fixed.*

Maybe one underlying dynamic we need to think about is the possibility that our lifestyles—our noises and our gadgets—have disconnected us from the natural world so much that we often just forget to care. What do you think about that?

How do you think all the daily noise in our air affects our ability to care about one another? To care about Earth?

Wrap up with a statement of purpose about the *Breathe* journey and invite the girls to add their own thoughts. You might say something like: *Breathe is our space to become more aware of what we value and care deeply enough about to act on, and then alert others to act, too. At the same time, we'll enjoy creating a little space in our lives so that we are clearheaded about who we are and what we value. So* Breathe *is about air for Earth, and airtime for us!*

SOUNDS OF NATURE

Perhaps you or one of the girls has music that simulates rain, the ocean, or other nature sounds. You may even have a rain stick. If the group is interested, use these to jump-start thinking about the sounds of Earth.

Journey Logistics

Encourage the girls to tailor this journey to their particular interests and needs. Tell them if there are any time constraints upon you. Ask them for theirs. If you all have plenty of time, say: *We can take as much time as you need and wish to complete the activities and awards, and explore your interest.*

Opening and Closing Ceremonies: Explain that the opening and closing moments of each session are a way for the team to mark gatherings as special and different from the routines of our days. Encourage girls to share their ideas for these ceremonies and for the celebrations and foods you will share along the journey.

Awards Along the Journey: Talk to the girls about the AWARE, ALERT, and AFFIRM awards as detailed on pages 102–106 of their books. Let them know that if they want to earn the awards, many of the steps can be incorporated into the team's gatherings.

Special Add-Ons: Talk to the girls about any field trips or outings that they might like to do as part of *Breathe.* Is there interest in venturing outdoors? What does the team have the time and resources to plan and do? Ask the girls to volunteer for lead roles in planning any outings or events the group wants to consider.

Gearing Up for the Next *Breathe* Gathering: Do any girls want to volunteer to lead some or all of the next gathering? An opening or closing? Bring music that inspires or relaxes or has "air" in its lyrics? Make arrangements to chat with girl volunteers at the end of this meeting or by phone between gatherings.

Ask each girl to bring a "scenty" thing or two from nature that she likes. Request that no perfumes be brought (they tend not to be natural, and some girls may be allergic to their ingredients).

Also, talk to the girls about making a scented relaxation item for the next session. Is there interest in the bath bag or lotion on pages 44 and 45? Do the girls have another natural personal-care item they'd like to make? Or would they like to bake an aromatic treat together? Do some yoga exercises? Does anyone know a community member who might assist? Based on the team's interest, organize the girls to bring in the needed supplies.

Closing Ceremony: Tuning in

Invite the girls to take a minute to make a commitment to listening for a special sound and allowing it to remind them to tune into a value that they want to pay more attention to in their lives.

The template below is one the girls might want to use. You might suggest that they also jot their commitment in their book or on a scrap of paper that they can carry with them. You might say: *At the next gathering, you may want to trade commitments and try someone else's or just make another commitment for yourself.*

My Commitment to Tune In

This week, I will listen for the sound of

_____

and let it remind me to be more

_____ in my life.

I will listen for the sound of trees
or bushes rustling and let it remind me
to be thankful that trees and plants contribute
to the air I need!

I will listen for the sound of birds
and let it remind me that birds are counting on
me to protect their resources!

SAMPLE SESSION 2
Scent Sense

AT A GLANCE

Goal: Girls examine how scents in the air make them feel, and explore relaxation and breathing techniques. They begin to think about "yucky stuff" in their air and how it affects them and Earth. As the session ends, girls work together to plan for "airy science" at the next gathering.

- Opening Ceremony

- Tuning In

- Scent Sense

- Air-Quality Log

- Aromatic Flair

- Harvesting Particulates: What's Really in the Air

- Journey Logistics

- Closing Reflection

MATERIALS

- **Scent Sense:** Scented items, such as lemons and limes (see page 43); paper or cardboard; pens and markers.

- **Aromatic Flair:** Supplies for the relaxation project the girls have chosen (see pages 44–45).

- **Harvesting Particulates:** Cellophane tape.

PREPARE AHEAD

Read through this session and check out the "Bad Air Hurts (and Smells)" section of the girls' book (page 65). Depending on what the team will make, organize the supplies and also remind the girls and their Friends and Family Network about materials needed. Advise the Cadettes to steep the rose water the day before the gathering—perhaps a pair of girls can volunteer to do this.

If the girls will have time, also consider these options:

- **Scrumptious Scents:** Depending on interest and facilities, this is a great opportunity to cook up something with a scrumptious aroma that the Cadette team can enjoy making and eating together. The girls might consider éclairs (rich, but a special treat), using the recipe on pages 50–51 of their book, or other recipes the girls and their families suggest. Remember, it's not just the end result, but also the process of teaming up (who brings which ingredients, how the food gets made, etc.) that makes cooking and sharing food a great experience for Cadettes.

- **Deep Breathing:** Another option, depending on interest and "expert" availability, is for the girls to work with their Friends and Family Network to invite a guest who can engage them in some basic yoga, Pilates, or meditation techniques. Yoga, Pilates, and meditation all involve taking deep breaths—to clear the air inside us, and help us feel refreshed and energized. Alternatively, the girls might seek out an aromatherapist.

AS GIRLS ARRIVE

Chat with any assistants about their roles before and during the session.

Opening Ceremony

Start with something the girls have suggested or what they prefer at this moment. Possibilities include:

- Lighting a candle, sitting quietly together for five minutes, and then sharing any thoughts that came to mind.

- Listening to a song together (or even singing it)—ideally one with inspirational lyrics about nature.

- Looking at a beautiful photo of nature and saying one word each about the feeling(s) it inspires. Each girl might bring her own nature image to this session or an upcoming one and say why she chose it, the sounds and scents it brings to mind, and how the image makes her feel.

Tuning In

Invite girls to share if they tried to "tune in" to a particular Earth sound this week. Ask: *What do sounds remind us to value and care about? If we are in the habit of being mindful, will we be more likely to act based on our values?*

If the team is interested in continuing this practice, they might swap "tune in" notes or make new ones. Keep a jar of notes to choose from.

The girls might also enjoy sitting quietly together for a set period of time. Other traditions that encourage the girls to tune into silence and the sounds of nature might emerge throughout *Breathe* based on the Cadettes' interest.

BE PREPARED FOR GUESTS

When guests visit, be sure the girls seize the opportunity to ask questions toward earning their AWARE Award. The tips on page 11–13 of their book can guide them.

Scent Sense

Start off by saying something like: *Last week we concentrated on using our sense of sound. This week we're going to concentrate on our sense of smell by thinking about all the scents that travel through the air and into us.*

Invite the girls to arrange their "scenty" things in stations around the meeting space. At each station, put a blank piece of paper or cardboard and some markers. Ask the girls if they want quiet music played as they visit the stations. Dig into your own stash of scented stuff to supplement what the girls set up. Make sure there are enough stations so that only one or two girls are at a station at a time.

Guide a quick brainstorm of ways that scents make us feel—energized, happy, relaxed, etc.—just long enough to get those Cadette lightbulbs going. Then invite the girls to rotate through the stations, savoring each scent and jotting a few words, phrases, or doodles on the paper or cardboard to explain how the scent makes them feel.

DISCUSSION

After the girls have visited all the stations, reassemble the group and share the collages created by their words and images. Then get a discussion going. You might ask:

- *What scent do you like best of all? Why? How did it make you feel?*

- *Was there a scent you didn't like so much? Why?*

- *On an average day in your life, are you tuned into scents that make you feel good? Why or why not? Are you distracted and preoccupied? Is there too much else going on in our air?*

- *What unpleasant smells get in your way some days? Car exhaust? Cleaning products? Stinky gym clothes? Cigarettes? Stale air? Garbage?*

As the girls brainstorm, ask for a volunteer to list the scents on a "Yucky Stuff in Air" paper. (Save this for today's closing and also for Session 3.)

Now ask: *What if the air around us was more pure, more of the time? What would our lives be like if we smelled fresh air more often? Would we feel more clearheaded? How would it help people? Animals? Plants? The whole Earth?*

SCENT STATION SUGGESTIONS

- Slices of citrus fruits— lemons, limes, oranges— either together or at separate stations

- Peppermint tea or candy

- Cinnamon

- Vanilla extract

- Pinecones

- A jar of seawater

- Aromatic flowers (roses, honeysuckle, jasmine)

- Herbs (basil, cilantro, rosemary)

- Jars of essential oils (lavender, eucalyptus, tea tree)

- Natural soaps

Air-Quality Log

Ask the girls to check out the Compare Air log on pages 14–15 of their book. Take a minute so that they can start their logs. Encourage them to add to their logs between meetings. In other words, encourage them to get AWARE of all that is in the air—good and bad! If possible, invite the girls to step outside now for a few minutes to compare the indoor and outdoor air.

Aromatic Flair

As you engage the girls in making the scented item they have selected (a recipe, the bath bag, the lotion), or in the yoga or other exercises that your guest will lead, open up a discussion about stress.

Ask: *What stresses you out day to day?* Have the girls brainstorm a list of some of the issues that stress them out.

Suggest: *It's always important to make quiet time and space for yourself to de-stress a little and think about what you value and, based on that, how you might work through some of the problems that cause stress in your life. Does anyone have any good stress busters to share?*

Ask: *Have you tried the "Need Some Space?" suggestions from* Breathe*? Notice, for example, pages 27 and 81. Maybe you'll try some over the next few weeks.*

Find out if the girls have heard of aromatherapy, the practice of using essential oils from plants to promote emotional and psychological well-being.

Explain that this activity is a simple way to demonstrate that natural ingredients can be used for personal-care products—and for cleaning—as described in *Breathe*.

AROMATIC BATH BAG

Begin putting together the bath bags, mentioning that they make simple, pretty, and inexpensive gifts for friends and family.

Say: *These little bags will scent the water for two or three relaxing baths. The primary fragrance will be lavender, but an added touch of herbs may tickle your nose and your fancy, too. You can experiment here by sniffing, and continue the experiment at home until you find a scent that feels like you.*

- Have girls distribute the fabric squares. Say: *Natural ingredients are generally better for your health and less likely to cause allergic reactions than synthetic chemicals. Why do you think that is?*

MATERIALS

AROMATIC BATH BAG

- 8-inch by 8-inch square of fine cheesecloth or muslin for each girl

- a tablespoon of dried lavender for each

- some dried basil, rosemary, sage, or lemon verbena

- a cup of rolled oats or powdered milk, if desired

- twist ties and about 2 feet of ribbon for each girl

- stirring sticks

- Explain that the bath bags need to be made with 1 tablespoon of the main ingredient—lavender—and with smaller amounts (less than a teaspoonful) of other aromatic herbs, such as dried basil, chamomile, lemon verbena, rosemary, sage, thyme, or any mint.

- Say: *Some herbalists add small amounts of oatmeal or powdered milk to these products for their skin-soothing properties. People who could afford it used to take milk baths. Can you think why?* (Answer: *To smooth and soften their skin.*)

- Once the girls have added the lavender and the other herbs, invite them to mix the ingredients with their fingers.

- Instruct the girls to gather the ends of the fabric square together and tie them about halfway down with a rubber band or twist tie.

- Tie the ribbon around the fastening, making the loop wide enough that the girls can drape it around a bathtub faucet. That way, the bag will hang into the tub and scent the water.

- Tell the girls that the bags may be used until they no longer adequately scent the bathwater. (And, just like air, water needs care. So you might encourage the girls to thinks of baths as a luxury. They use more water than showers!)

ROSE AND LIME SCENTED LOTION

Making the rose water: The rose water must be made in advance (2 cups boiling water and 1 cup clean, packed rose petals—no stems or leaves— make enough for 16 girls). Ask a few girls to make enough for the team: Just steep the petals in the boiling water in a Pyrex dish or bowl (covered with a lid or plate), let it sit and cool for a day. Bring a strainer to the gathering.

Materials: Rose water (see directions above), glycerine, lime juice, small glass jar with lid, stirring sticks

- Instruct the girls to strain the rose water into a large cup or a small bowl. Instruct them to push and squeeze the rose petals to get all the water out.

- Ask: *Do you notice any rose oil on your skin? Most herbs and flowers have essential oils. Some are used in making expensive perfumes. Many of these oils, like jojoba, tea tree, and apricot, have healing properties.*

- Have each girl measure and pour her glycerine into her bottle. Then, have each girl add her lime juice while stirring the mixture with a stick. When adding the rose water, the girls should stir the fragrant water drops in slowly and consistently until all ingredients are blended.

- Encourage the girls to sample the mildly astringent lotion by rubbing a bit on their hands or forearms. Then they can tighten the lids, take the lotion home, and enjoy!

MATERIALS

ROSE AND LIME SCENTED LOTION

- Small glass jar with lid

- Stirring sticks

Each girl's portion of lotion will also require:

- 1 tablespoon glycerine (available at drugstores and health food stores)

- 2 tablespoons rose water (see directions at left)

- 1½ tablespoons lime juice

Harvesting Particulates: What's Really in the Air?

Before the gathering wraps up, engage the girls in this simple science project, which measures particulates in the air in and around their meeting place. The girls will place pieces of tape face up on a windowsill, countertop, and other indoor and outdoor places, and then check the tape at the next session. (If leaving the tape in place is not possible, encourage the girls to try the experiment at home, following the steps on page 68 of their book.)

Say: *We've been using our senses to get our minds on air. We've also been doing some science via the recipes we have been following.*

At our next gathering, we'll dive into some fun science experiments so that we can be more AWARE of the science of air. We'll start today by setting up a little experiment to explore what's in our air!

BEING AIR AWARE

The girls might want to try this experiment anywhere else they spend a lot of time.

- Ask the girls if they've ever seen stuff in the air: *Do you ever remember seeing soot or fine dirt accumulate outside? Have you seen acid rain leave a residue on leaves?*

- Explain that "particulate matter" can be a fine dust from carbon-based fuels like coal and oil, or larger particles like soot. You might say: *It is one of the components of air pollution, and now we're going to harvest some using a simple piece of cellophane tape.*

- Ask the girls to break into two-person teams to think of a few places where they might position their tape. You might say: *Where could we safely attach some tape face-up to grab particulates?* (The outside of windowsills or a door frame would work, or the back of outdoor furniture.)

- Instruct each team to place a 6-inch strip of tape, sticky side up, on a few inside and outside spots. They should fix the tape at each end with smaller pieces, sticky side down. Suggest: *Let's try some spaces high up and down low, too. Then we can see if there's a difference in the air.*

- When the tapes have been secured, say: *Now remember the location of your tape so you can examine it at our next gathering.*

Journey Logistics

Invite the girls to check out the options for science projects for the next gathering (pages 50–56 in this guide). Which interest them most? Find out who can help bring in and set up the various supplies (most are household items). And who might like to be in charge of the science stations?

Also, get a brainstorm going about "air experts" who could join the team for the next session. Does anyone know a science teacher who might like to visit? Have contacts at a local college? Refer to the AWARE list in the girls' Award Tracker (page 103 of their book). Encourage girls to do some of the inviting themselves. Also, encourage them to consider the kinds of questions they might like to ask guest experts, referring to pages 11–13 of their book. Talking to people who have an interest in air is a step toward earning Aware!

This is also a good time to check in on any other planning regarding an outdoor outing or trip the girls are interested in before the journey ends.

Closing Reflection

Ask the team to gather into a circle. Briefly mention themes explored on the journey so far, by saying something like: *We have been using our senses of sound and smell to become more aware of:*

- noises in the air
- using silence to connect us to one another and to sounds we love in nature
- the scents we enjoy breathing in the air
- scents that are yucky!

On a day-to-day basis, we probably don't usually think much about air. Why not? (Possible answers: *It's free! You can't really see it or touch it! It's just always there.*)

Now invite a girl to read the first two lines of the *Breathe* book:

You might live 40 days without food and three days without water. But you'll only last about eight minutes without air.

Pass around the "Yucky Stuff in the Air" list the team created during today's activity on scents. Individually, or as a team, the girls might make a *Breathe* mission statement, capturing in a short phrase—T-shirt or bumper-sticker size—their reason for caring for air.

COACHING TIPS: TEAMWORK

Keep in mind that logistics planning time is not just about "getting things done." It offers great opportunities for girls to team up and also to try out new challenges by volunteering for different aspects of upcoming gatherings. So, keep your eyes and ears open for opportunities to coach girls, including:

- Drawing out girls who might be hanging back to see what "flair" they have that they can share with the team.

- Inviting girls to make observations about their team efforts by asking questions: *How do you think you are doing as a team? What works really well? What teamwork areas could you strengthen?*

SAMPLE SESSION 3
What's in the Air?

AT A GLANCE

Goal: Girls engage in hands-on science experiments to gain awareness of the wonders of air. They use their increased awareness to team up and develop an observational tool to work with at their next gathering.

- Opening Ceremony: AWARE!
- Relaxed?
- AIRY Science
- Planning for Air Care Field Observation
- Closing Reflection: Sharpen Your Vision!

MATERIALS

- **AIRY Science:** magnifying glasses to see particulates; whatever else the girls need for the various science experiments(s) they've selected (see pages 50–56).

PREPARE AHEAD

- Read through the "Airy Science" experiments (pages 51-55), and based on the girls' input, choose those that seem most interesting to the team. The girls may also enjoy fitting a science experiment or two into upcoming gatherings, rather than doing them all at once.

- Find out if any girls are interested in leading the science experiments. Plan to set up stations so that girls can rotate through them. That way, everyone will have a chance to be in on the action.

- Follow up on the possibility of having a guest or two attend to lend some "airy insights" during the session. See the tips on pages 11–13 of the girls' book, and encourage girls to do some of the inviting! Note that talking with experts is a step to the AWARE Award. Girls can ask some questions, using the tips on pages 11–13 to get the conversation going!

OPENING OPTIONS

Depending on the energy level and interest of the girls, other options for beginning the session might include:

- Sharing some deep breaths and moments of silence
- Continuing the "Tuning In" exercise
- Enjoying a few minutes of cardio fun together (dancing, a trip up and down stairs . . .)
- Observing the air and adding notes to their Compare Air logs about the air in and outside the meeting space

- If your time permits, you might practice an experiment or two at home to boost your confidence. Check out "The Amazing Pressure of Air" on page 54. You'll feel like a magician!

Opening Ceremony

Maybe girls have planned one! Consider using this opening to pick up where the team left off last time: their mission for *Breathe*. Gather the team together around their mission statement (if they are still thinking about one, that's OK). Say something like:

Breathe is an opportunity to create airspace for us, and to figure out how to improve air quality for Earth. To do that means being more AWARE!

Then invite each girl to say one way she is becoming more AWARE about what goes on in her own airspace or the air around her—or both!

If the team is feeling "arty," they might like to capture their statements in a group collage or poem, now or at a later time.

Relaxed?

Ask the girls whether they are trying out any of the relaxation techniques shared (or made) at the last gathering.

You can try questions like: *How did it feel? Have aromas helped you relax and unwind? Does the power of scent tell you anything you didn't know about air? About air quality? Have you been logging air-quality observations? What have you noticed?*

Have the group consider how air affects all our senses—hearing, smelling, touching, seeing, and even taste. Ask: *What do you taste in "bad" air? In good air? Think about that as you continue your journey.*

AIRY Science

Say: *Today's science investigations will engage us in more air AWAREness. We'll be seeing some unique properties of air. Let's start by checking in on what's happened with our pieces of tape since our last meeting.*

- Ask the girls to organize themselves back into their "particulate teams" and remember where they placed their pieces of tape.
- Ask one of the girls to give each team an index card and a piece of

notebook paper for harvesting the particulates. Say: *When you find each piece of tape, turn it over and tape it down on a white index card or piece of paper. You can see the larger particles you've collected with your eyes, and you'll see even more with a magnifying glass.*

- Say: *When you measure and compare the particles, be sure to use a defined area. Place a hole in a piece of notebook paper over the tape, then count the particles you can see with your eye or magnifying glass or the microscope. This will give you an idea of how much dust, soot, and other particulate pollution you might be breathing in.*

- Instruct each team to record the number of particles in that defined area for an indoor and outdoor piece of tape. Is there a difference between two? Between different parts of the room? Different heights?

Then get going on any other experiment stations the girls have chosen to try, following these step-by-step instructions:

AIR IS HERE, THERE, AND EVERYWHERE

1 Turn on the fan. If there are ceiling fans, turn those on, too, and have the girls move closer. Say something like: *Can you see the air now?* Depending on the light, they may be able to see the air moving in front of the fan.

2 Then you might say: *Can you feel the air? How does it feel?* Encourage them to enjoy the breeze and think about what's in it.

3 If no one has mentioned the word "wind" yet, you might say: *What's moving air called?*

4 Keep the discussion going by asking the girls to name the times and ways they've experienced wind.

- *when it clears the air*

- *when it messes my hair*

- *when a hurricane hits or dry winds fan fires*

- *When I go sailing*

5 Encourage the girls to check out the "Feeling the Wind at Your Back" section of their book starting on page 90, which focuses on how wind can be harnessed as a sustainable, alternative form of energy: wind power.

WHAT YOU NEED:

- a small fan

LIGHTWEIGHT CHAMPION

WHAT YOU NEED:

- a few balloons
- straws or pencils
- pieces of string

1 Using a straw or a pencil as a balancing "scale," instruct the girls to tape a piece of string or thread to the middle of the straw or pencil. Ask one girl to hold the string. Make sure that the straw or pencil is balanced.

2 Ask the girls to tape an uninflated balloon to each end of the straw or pencil. Make sure that the straw or pencil remains level. Say: *This is our balance scale.*

3 Next ask a girl to remove one of the balloons, inflate it, and tie it off. Ask another girl to retape it to the balance scale, with the uninflated balloon still on the other side. Say: *Let's observe what happens to the scale.*

4 When the girls have made their observations, ask: Can you balance the inflated and the uninflated balloons? Why not? Which balloon is heavier?

Though you don't usually feel it, air definitely has weight! When have you felt it?

NO EMPTY SPACE: AIR HAS MASS

WHAT YOU NEED:

- a see-through glass or plastic pitcher
- paper towels
- a 6- to 8-inch glass that fits inside the pitcher

1 Have a girl fill the pitcher with about 2 inches of water.

2 Ask another girl to stuff a wad of paper towels into the bottom of the glass, tight enough that it doesn't fall out when the glass is turned upside down. The wad of paper towels should be no more than an inch or two thick.

3 Now ask the girls to turn the glass upside-down and put it into the pitcher of water. Ask: *What do you observe? At first the girls might say, "Nothing." The paper should remain stuck in the glass.* Ask again: *What do you observe?*

4 If no one mentions that the paper stays dry, ask a girl to remove the glass from the pitcher and the paper from the glass. Pass the paper towel around so everyone realizes it is dry. Then ask a girl to stuff the paper back into the glass, and return the glass to the pitcher. Ask: *Why does the paper towel stay dry?*

The water doesn't rise to meet the paper towel because the air between the towel and the water takes up space. Air has mass; it takes up space—something we rarely think about.

5 Keep guiding the discussion as long as the girls have something to say. The concept of "something we rarely think about" is important to girls gaining AWAREness about air on Earth! You might ask: *How does taking air for granted contribute to poor air quality?*

HOW MUCH OF AIR IS OXYGEN?

Here's an experiment girls can try at home using simple materials. If several girls are interested (or all of them!), they can compare measurements. Remind the girls: *Oxygen is the element in air that sustains life. Do you wonder how much oxygen is in the air? This activity will answer that question.*

Then give the girls these instructions:

1 Put a wad of steel wool inside the jar. Explain that they need to use enough so that when they stuff it into the jar and turn the jar upside down, the wool stays stuck inside, just like the paper towel did. Say: *Be sure that the wad of steel does not fall out when you turn the jar upside down.*

2 Fill a flat-bottomed bowl or dish half full of water.

3 Put the jar upside-down into the water. Put some pebbles under the rim of the jar to lift it so water can get in easily. The water will come up into the jar.

4 Mark the level of the water in the jar with a grease pencil.

5 When you've determined whether the experiment will be taken home by a Cadette or kept in your gathering space, say: *It would be good to check this setup every day and record what you observe. You'll notice the water will rise higher than the water in the dish and the steel wool will have become rusty. Mark how high the water rises. Why did this happen?*

6 The difference between the two marks represents how much oxygen was in the air in the jar. Invite the girls to figure this out on their own by asking questions such as: *Why did the steel wool get rusty? Why was the water able to rise in the jar?*

WHAT YOU NEED:

- glass jar
- wad of steel wool
- flat-bottomed bowl or dish half full of water.

WHAT'S RUST?

Rust is a combination of steel (iron, actually) and oxygen.

In this experiment, the rust that forms uses up all the oxygen in the air in the jar. The water then flows in to take the place of the oxygen.

THE INCREDIBLE COLLAPSING MILK JUG

WHAT YOU NEED:

- empty plastic gallon milk jugs with screw-on tops

- hot water from the tap or a kettle.

NOTE

The girls observe what is happening 30–60 minutes after they set up the experiment.

1 Gather the girls around the empty milk jugs with screw-on tops and ask a girl to record the team's responses and observations.

2 If tap water can get hot enough, ask the girls to pour in water until the jugs are about one-quarter full. (Or use a kettle and a pot holder.)

3 Tell each team to cap its jug tightly and let the "experiment" sit while they move on to the next activity. Ask the recorder to jot down the time.

Before you begin the next activity, say: *What do you expect to happen with the jugs?* Ask the recorder to jot down some responses. Wait at least half an hour before asking the girls to make observations; do so again closer to an hour later, if possible.

4 When you and the girls return to observe the jugs, you might say: *Why don't each of you say what happened?* The milk jug will have crumpled in on itself.

5 As the girls attempt to determine why this happened, take them back to the hot water. You might say: *When you added the hot water, what did it do to the air temperature inside the jug?*

6 If one of the girls says that the temperature rose and the hot air expanded, say: *Exactly. Once you sealed the jug, no air could get in or out. Hot air expands and so the jug did, too.*

7 Encourage the girls to move to the next step. Ask: *What happened inside the jug when the air cooled off?* (Answer: *The cooled air caused the pressure inside the jug to decrease. As the pressure on the inside walls of the jug decreased, the walls of the jug collapsed. There wasn't enough air pressure inside the jug to offset the air pressure on the outside of the jug.*)

THE AMAZING PRESSURE OF AIR

WHAT YOU NEED:

- tub or bucket

- plastic cup

- water

- index card or lid from cottage cheese container

This activity may require a little advance practice so you can guide the girls more effectively. Once you've demonstrated how to remove your hand gently enough that the lid stays stuck to the cup, invite the girls to attempt it, too.

1 Place the tub or bucket on a table or gather the girls around a sink to catch any spills from the experiment

2 Fill the plastic cup almost to the top with water.

3 Place the index card or cottage cheese lid over the mouth of the cup and situate it over the sink or bucket.

4 While holding the lid tightly in place with one hand, gently hold the cup in the other and turn it upside down over the sink or tub.

5 When the cup is completely upside down, slowly remove your hand from the index card or lid. The lid should stay stuck underneath the overturned cup.

You might say, *What did you observe and why do you think that happened?*

The girls might think there's a trick involved at first.

Say: *The only trick is to remove your hand gently enough that the lid stays stuck to the cup.*

6 Encourage the girls to organize into two-person teams to attempt the demonstration on their own.

- Give the teams plenty of time for each person to master the art of not dropping the index card or plastic lid.

- Encourage the girls who have succeeded to give tips to those still having trouble getting the card or lid to stay put.

- When everyone has had enough tries to feel how the card or lid remains in place, ask the girls to join in a discussion about the experiment.

7 To start, you might ask: *As you removed your hand from the lid, could you FEEL what is happening? Air pressure, though invisible, pushes up and holds the lid in place, counteracting the pressure of the water coming down on it.*

8 If time and space allow, invite the girls to try again with larger and smaller cups and lids. Encourage them to observe the differences and discuss what accounts for them.

9 Guide the discussion toward the process of trial and error itself. Say something like: *Isn't it great that no matter how hard a skill seems at first, once you've done it right, you can feel your way toward doing it right again?*

10 Once they've mastered the experiment, remind them that this is an activity that they can practice and will enjoy showing to their families.

AWE THEM WITH AIR

These experiments ground the Cadettes in scientific facts and also let them have some fun with the mystery and magic of air!

As they consider which experiments to try, you might say, *Soon you will see that air pressure seems invisible. These experiments have an aura of mystery and magic.*

Little brothers and sisters will think you've mastered quite a trick! And think how good it feels to master a new skill and then to share it with others!

Planning for Air Care Field Observation

After everyone has had a chance to explore the various experiment stations, call the girls together to develop an observation checklist for use in next session's field visit. If any of the girls have laptops or if there is a computer available where you meet, they might use them to create their observation tool. Otherwise, a handwritten observation is just fine!

Guide the girls to create a list of what to observe about the air quality—inside and outside. Give them some hints. They could develop the list by:

- Checking out all the topics and tidbits in their *Breathe* books—the "aerial view" on page 3 is a great place to start.

- Looking back at their "Yucky Stuff in Air" list from Session 2.

- Looking at their Compare Air logs

- Getting a little guidance from you, via the list below! But before you provide these suggestions, see what the girls come up with on their own. And don't worry: They don't have to list every item here. More might occur to them during their fieldwork.

- Using some of their insights from their experiments. What else might the girls want to observe or try doing while they are out and about?

OUTDOOR SUGGESTIONS

- Noise: What kinds do they hear? How might it affect the air?

- Idling cars or buses and the noise and fumes they produce

- Cigarette smoke or butts

- Quantity and health of trees and plants

- Evidence of wasted paper

- Garbage (and the smells it produces)

- Fertilizers, pesticides, or other chemicals in use (or evidence that they have been in use)

INDOOR SUGGESTIONS

Share this fact: *Several of the women profiled in the girls' book study the atmosphere both indoors and outdoors. All agree that pollution is greater indoors than outdoors in most places!*

- Is the air around you clean or dusty?

- Are any cleaning supplies the kind that hurt the air?

- Do any cracks let in leaks and cause dampness that leads to mold?

- Is there mildew in rugs or upholstery?

OPTION: AIR AND HEALTH

Depending on girl interests, instead of (or in addition to) the field observation, girls might like to dive into public health concerns related to smoking or asthma. If this is the team's preference, they can spend time here:

- Deciding whom they could interview to learn more

- Planning a visit to a local health provider, an office of public health, etc.

- Brainstorming questions to ask to learn more about the problem and possible solutions

- Are there any plants?

- Cigarette butts, ashes, or smoke?

- Do street noises or fumes come in through windows and doors?

- Is there wasted paper or an insufficient recycling plan?

Ask the girls how they might best set up their questions and issues for use during the fieldwork. A chart like the one on the next page might be useful. The girls could return to it as they focus in on an ALERT project in Session 5.

INFORMAL INTERVIEWS

Encourage the girls to think of some questions they can ask people while they are out observing. This is a chance for them to find out how AWARE other people are about air issues. Possible questions might include:

- What times of the day or the week does traffic idle here? What do you think happens to the fumes?

- Do you see people smoking here often? Where do the butts and the smoke go? How does it affect you? Others?

- Would you like to see more greenery here? Why? What would it take?

WHERE TO CONDUCT THE OBSERVATION

End by making a team decision about where to hold the next gathering. Ideally, the girls will conduct their observation in a place where they can explore both indoors and outdoors, such as a school and its grounds, an office complex, a few city blocks, a mall, or a movie theater or supermarket and its adjoining parking lot. When on location, the girls might talk to a few people, asking the questions they developed. Plan to have enough adults on hand to ensure the girls' safety, should they fan out in small groups.

Closing Reflection: Sharpen Your Vision!

Gather the girls in a circle and read them this passage from the first Cadette Girl Scout Handbook, written in 1963. The team might find it particularly inspirational as they look ahead to their observational outing:

"A fascinating outdoor world is waiting for you to explore it. Full of beauty, it offers many treasures . . . Your chief instruments of exploration are your senses. Sharpen your vision, your observations. Record what you see for your enjoyment and the pleasure of others."

After you read it, ask the girls: *Now, what do you hope to explore? What might you record? If you find unpleasant aspects of air, how might you come up with ways to turn them into pleasant and pleasurable ones?*

GIRL LED, WITH FLAIR!

Depending on the group's time and transportation, the girls could opt to conduct observations on their own, or in small teams, between now and the next gathering. They could, for example, scope out their schools and other buildings they and their families frequent, and then share their observations at the next team gathering.

Ask the girls how they might like to creatively document their observations. Perhaps they can bring a camera or a video or tape recorder. Invite girls to add their flair to this exploration. Who is good with words and would like to write a story about the team's adventure? Create a photojournal? Interview some people?

Finally, discuss the possibility of inviting a local professional who can lend some "airy" expertise to your observational trip. Perhaps someone from the county department of health or a local environmental conservation organization? The meteorologist from a local television or radio station? A contact from a science or public health department at a university?

AWARE Observations

Possible air care issue	Evidence observed	Why this is an issue	What is the impact on Earth? On us?	What could we do about it?

SAMPLE SESSION 4
Get AWARE

AT A GLANCE

Goal: Girls conduct their air observations or public health exploration and interviews and add to their Compare Air logs. Along the way, they think about the flair they have as individuals and as a team. They consider their reasons for caring about air. They might even be ready to earn their AWARE award.

- **Get AWARE: Observational Trip**
- **Closing Ceremony**

MATERIALS

- **Get AWARE:** Observation tools girls created in Session 3; pen and paper; cameras or other equipment girls want to use for documenting the observation.

PREPARE AHEAD

- Refresh yourself on the air-quality topics throughout the girls' book so you can assist the Cadettes to think about air during the observation.

- Depending upon where the group will meet, arrange transportation and adult helpers via the Friend and Family Network. Also, confirm any special guests who have agreed to talk with girls during the observation.

AS GIRLS ARRIVE

Talk with any assistants about their roles before and during the field trip. If small teams fan out, trade cell phone numbers and make sure each group has an adult assistant.

Get AWARE: Observational Trip

Gather up and head to the location chosen for the observational exploration so the team can get AWARE of how air might need care in their area. Bring along the observational tool the girls created at the last gathering and the gadgets they want to use to document their observations or interviews (cameras, tape recorders, etc.).

Remind the girls to stop occasionally during their fieldwork to note what they see, hear, feel, smell, and taste in the air for their Compare Air logs.

Depending on the group size and number of adult assistants available, the group might split into small teams. Each will tackle all or some of the items on the list the team developed.

ADD IN SOME FLAIR!

Add a fun challenge to the outing by encouraging the girls to observe their individual and team flair during the outing. Who is creative? Who is practical? Who keeps the team on track? Suggest that girls observe one another's flair so that at an upcoming gathering, they can "award" it.

Designate a place and time for the team(s) to regroup. You can talk in detail about the observations at your next gathering, but before the team goes home for the day, take a few minutes to:

- Share any highs and lows from the effort. Ask: *Was it hard or easy to observe air-quality issues?* If the girls found it hard, remind them why: *Air is all around us, so it can be hard to touch and see! It's hard to get people to think about it, too!*

- Ask: *Did you meet or talk to anyone who had ideas about air? Was it hard for them? Do people in general take air for granted? Why?*

- Provide encouragement—it's hard to get our hearts and minds around air!

- Ask if the girls have any new flair highlights to share!

Closing Ceremony

Let the team know that they have made excellent progress toward earning their AWARE awards—and perhaps even completed all the steps! Encourage the team to check out the steps on the Award Tracker on page 103 of their book. What do they have left to do? If they have not yet talked to some experts, what ideas do they have about doing so?

Note that the last step to earning AWARE is for each girl to write a personal statement about why she cares about air, one that she will share with the rest of the team. The girls can do this now, as their closing, or opt to do so at the opening of their next gathering.

If they need a little assistance to get going, ask a few questions, like these:

- *What have you become more aware of related to air in our lives since* Breathe *started?*
- *What matters to you: Making more quiet time to tune into ourselves and nature? Dealing with the source of smells that are bad for us to breathe in? Trying to prevent kids from smoking? Making sure we have more plants and trees?*
- *Why do these things matter to you? Why be AWARE and care?*
- *Isn't it interesting how what is good for Earth is good for us, too?*

Consider also using the closing today to engage girls in thinking about all the interesting education and career possibilities available to them. There are so many to gain AWAREness of!

Suggest they flip through their book for a few minutes and select their favorite from among the women and girls doing something for Earth. Then, ask the girls to say a few words about what new possibilities the story makes them AWARE of and why they are intrigued. You can do this as a large group or in small teams.

In addition to thinking about the women featured in their book, girls could also think about what they have learned from any guests they have networked with during *Breathe* gatherings, or stories they are AWARE of in the news.

SAMPLE SESSION 5
ALERT Who About What?

AT A GLANCE

Goal: The girls assess what they learned during their observational visit, and their reasons for caring about air. They use their insights to make a team decision on an ALERT project and begin planning it together.

- Opening Ceremony: Earning AWARE
- Observing the Observations
- Choosing an ALERT
- Journey Logistics
- Animal Sense
- Closing Ceremony

MATERIALS

- **Opening Ceremony:** The girls' book; AWARE awards.
- **Observing the Observations:** Paper and pens; observations from field visit.

PREPARE AHEAD

Check out all the examples of Alert projects in the girls' book. You'll be guiding them to choose a project to educate and inspire others to act for improved air quality. As you do this, remember:

- The ALERT project is an opportunity for girls to educate and inspire others to join them in Taking Action for air. So they need to identify and organize an Air Care Team—not just plan to Take Action on their own.

- The ALERT project can be big or small, depending on the team's interests and resources. What matters is that the girls are able to: (a) try engaging others, (b) develop and implement a plan, (c) explore sustainable—not one-shot—solution-building.

AS GIRLS ARRIVE

Chat with any assistants about their roles before and during the session.

Opening Ceremony: Earning AWARE

Perhaps girls have planned something or want to continue a tradition of quiet time or sharing how they have been "Tuning In." Or you might read this quote attributed to a fifth-grade teacher and ask the girls to say a few words about what it means to them:

> *"Life is not measured by the number of breaths we take, but by the moments that take our breath away."*

If the team has completed the steps to earning the AWARE award (page 102–103 in their book), they might like to begin with a little ceremony as they receive the award. Suggest a few minutes of quiet time for girls to write their statements about why they care about Earth's air (the last step to earning the award). Then encourage the girls to share their ideas with each other.

Wrap up by congratulating the girls for earning this award. You might say: *Leaders learn to be AWARE of what goes on in the world around them. Right now we are concentrating on air, but you can use your AWARE award to remind yourself that you strive to be AWARE of all that matters in your world!*

Observing the Observations

Get the girls started on a discussion about what they observed during their field exploration. Here are some discussion prompts to get the team going:

- *What did you notice that surprised you? Did you observe anything that you had never really thought about before?*

- *What did you notice that says something positive about the air we breath? What did you notice that could be a sign of air-quality issues?*

- *Did you see any signs of cigarette smoking?*

- *What noises were in the air that were bothersome? Did you hear any nature noises you'd like to hear more of?*

- *What senses did you engage?*

- *Who did you talk to? What did you learn from them? What did the conversations make you think about?*

TIPS FOR SHARING AND DISCUSSING

As the girls say their "cares," they might make broad statements like "smoking causes cancer" and "idling trucks, buses, and cars stink." Encourage them to try to personalize why they care. Ask: *How does this affect you and your well-being? Your health? Others? Earth?*

As you keep working with the girls, remind them to practice expressing their "cares" to inspire—because that leads others to care. You might say: *If you can convey a personal impact and your own passion, it will be easier for others to care, too. Here are examples of personalized statements:*

"The asthma epidemic is getting worse. My sister has asthma, and I want to do something about the environmental triggers in our home and neighborhood, so she'll have fewer asthma attacks."

"All that loud media static out there affects my ability to pay attention. When I can't concentrate, I can't be a good student or a good friend."

Choosing an ALERT

Transition the team into thinking about their ALERT project. You might say: *Now that we are more and more AWARE of air and why we care, we are going to choose a project that ALERTs others to care and to get involved, too.*

Suggest that the team check out the ALERT information and steps in their Award Tracker on pages 104–105 of their book.

GUIDING QUESTIONS

Before the team starts brainstorming, coach them to set up some "Guiding Questions" (like those in the chart below) for an ALERT project that will be meaningful and have a positive impact. You can start with these suggestions and see what others the girls can add. The girls will ask themselves these questions as they develop their project ideas and plans. Explain that if they can't answer the questions, an idea might not be a viable project!

Guiding Questions	Hints
What is a specific action we and others can take that will have an impact?	We need to isolate an issue—and even break it down to one area—so that it is specific enough to have a tangible "call to action" that we can ask others to join us in carrying out.
Who are the people we need to mobilize? How will we use what we have become AWARE of to educate and inspire them?	We will need to involve others to be on the Air Care Team to hear our ALERT and to go on and act!
Does this project inspire and motivate us? Will we be able to use our team and individual flair to see it through?	We want to be excited about the issue and the plan we choose, so that we will see it through!
Is this project realistic based on our time and other resources?	We want to create a project that is doable with the resources and time we have available.
How could this project affect air quality even after we sound the ALERT?	We want to strive toward a sustainable, lasting impact on air care.

TEAM BRAINSTORM AND DECISIONS

Now that girls have some Guiding Questions about what will make for a great project, invite them to have a team brainstorm and then make a group decision about one air issue they want to tackle as a team by ALERTing others about it and engaging them in solving it.

Get the brainstorm going and keep it moving by encouraging girls to think over everything they have learned and observed about air by:

- Reflecting back on their "Why Care?" statements. What do they have in common? Have any issues been repeated by many team members?

- Going over their observation documentation. What possibilities pop out?

- Going through their book together, looking at the issues and examples of what others are doing and what might be possible.

You might suggest that the girls create or adapt a chart like the one below to collect their ideas as they brainstorm.

Invite a girl to volunteer to guide the team to a decision. She could, for example:

- Post the key ideas that emerge on a big piece of paper.

- Ask for team members to give pros and cons of each—then see if any can be eliminated or if one rises up to first choice.

- Encourage the team to evaluate ideas using their Guiding Questions.

COACHING TIP:

If the girls have a hard time coming up with ideas, offer some prompts from this issue list to get the lightbulbs going:

- the health effects of air pollution

- the asthma epidemic

- toxic chemicals and their green alternatives

- the effects of smoking and secondhand smoke

- greening your school or community to improve air quality

- working toward less paper waste in school or elsewhere

- idling trucks, buses, and cars

- noise pollution and its impact on health

- silence—creating more of it in life

Air issue	What could be done	Whom would we need?	Pros	Cons	Potential impact

SCALING AND SCOPING!

You'll find descriptions of what ALERT projects might look like on pages 68–69. These have been summarized from the girls' book for your convenience as you advise the team on shaping their project.

As the girls' list comes into focus, ask them to consider practical issues. How much time can they focus on their effort? What assistance might they need? If the girls have a whole year and lots of interest, they might go all out with plans for a green roof or garden. If they have less time, their ALERT might focus on asking the school district to commit to starting plans for a garden or another project, or adding plants to every classroom.

You'll want the girls to feel that their ALERT project is successful, and success begins with a realistic project plan. Remember: Even small projects done with limited time can have an impact when they're well focused!

A VISION STATEMENT

Conclude the selection of an ALERT project by asking the girls to create a team vision statement for their effort. This template can get them started!

Vision Statement

As the Girl Scout **Cadettes** of _____,

we care about_____.

This matters to us because _____.

We plan to have an impact by organizing other people, like _____

_____.

We will educate and inspire them on the issue and then ask them

to take action by _____.

The impact we hope to have is _____

_____.

Journey Logistics

Let the girls know that during the next group gathering they will focus on how they plan to reach out to an Air Care Team and inspire them to act on their air issue.

- Will they hold a special event? Create a mascot? Use a poem, a song, or a skit?
- How might they use the documentation they gathered and created during their field observation?
- Is there anything from the sounds and scents and science sessions that might help engage the senses of others?
- What flair can each girl bring to the effort?

Based on the plan that has started to take shape, talk to the girls about rounding up the supplies and people they may need.

Also, take time to check in on other plans the group has been working on for an outing or a special event. How are those plans going? Who needs to do what?

And find out if anyone wants to lead a special "airy" opening or closing at the next gathering!

Animal Sense

After all the thinking work the team has done, if time permits, the girls might enjoy using their imaginations in a quick exercise about animals.

Encourage them to check out: "Hares, Mares, Bears! Oh, My!" in their books on page 62 and make an airy animal list just for fun. Or consider the information on the unique sensory powers of some animals on page 109. What would girls do with their heightened senses?

Closing Ceremony

Gather the team in a circle and invite each girl to "award" the girl on her left for the special flair she brings to the team. Examples might be: *I award you "Most Creative" because you . . . I award you "Team Energy Booster" because you . . .*

If the girls want to, they can write their Flair Awards in one another's *Breathe* books, or on a little notecard or scrap of paper that can be pasted in later.

After each girl has given and received a "Flair Award," say: *We all love to have our positive qualities appreciated! So, let's keep them coming—and maybe even take time during your life to do this with family and friends.*

ALERT Project Possibilities

CLEARING THE AIR AT SCHOOL

DETOX YOUR SCHOOL (OR SCHOOL DISTRICT)

This will involve research into what kind of cleaning supplies and pesticides the school uses; reaching out to administrative staff and perhaps a contracted cleaning company; and creating buzz around the issue by educating students and parents. Ultimately, the Air Care Team the girls have mobilized could propose the introduction of new approaches—or ask the school administration to adapt a three-year plan to take steps to change!

NO-IDLING ZONE

If the girls have noticed exhaust invading their classrooms and school grounds or other places in which they spend time, or have recorded complaints about exhaust enveloping the entire neighborhood around the school, this might be their project. After they check out the suggestions for de-fuming in their *Breathe* book, they'll be ready to influence the school administration, the school district, the block association, or maybe even the entire town to do something about fumes from idling school buses and cars.

GETTING GREEN WITH PLANTS

The positive effect of plants on air quality, personal health, and psychological well-being is also something the girls can read about in their book. Greenery can also screen ugly or distracting sights outside classroom windows, plus help buffer noise. If the girls launch an indoor greening project for their school, they may reach out to students, school administrators, and community members, sounding a green ALERT about plants and their benefits. Not able to do it at school? Where else in the community would more plants be useful?

ANTISMOKING PROJECTS

NO-BUTT ZONES

Because many middle schools are adjacent to a high school or commercial zone where people smoke and the girls have read some of the statistics about the health effects of secondhand smoke, they may decide to take action in this area. After they research the subject, they can reach out to school staff, the medical community, and the local office of the American Lung Association. To kick off their advocacy, the girls may want to organize a Smokers Be-W-Air fair, with booths offering various experiments and activities that highlight the hazards of smoking. They might also survey how nonsmokers feel about their friends who smoke and use their findings to create a media campaign in their school.

PERMANENT PAPER REDUCTION

CONSERVATION AND GREENING

The girls could start in their own classrooms by connecting with teachers to begin weighing the amount of paper used every week. They can check out deforestation and related topics in their book and then make the case for keeping forests healthy by reducing the amount of paper their school and its affiliated organizations use. They might even kick off the campaign with a Healthy Forests Week that includes different daily activities and a talk by an expert such as a Park Service worker or an arborist. The girls can keep weighing, stacking, and recording the results for a month or longer. They might even be able to make these new habits permanent—and communitywide.

NOISE POLLUTION ALERT

NOISE AND MEDIA

Starting with their personal noise logs, the girls begin keeping track of all the noise that distracts them in class or prevents a neighborhood from getting a good night's sleep. After accumulating that data and researching how to register complaints with agencies that can help, the girls take this forward into advocacy and get an entire school, neighborhood, or city to commit to reducing noise pollution. It could start with a day or period every month that gets a special "Quiet Focus." A community tip sheet and a strong ALERT might even lead to policy changes, like an antinoise ordinance that is enforced.

MEDIA MANNERS MANUAL

Are cell phones and text messages a huge distraction in the girls' lives? They may want to brainstorm an "etiquette manual" (one that uses paper wisely! could it be online?) to come up with ways to stay connected while still respecting others and keeping noise down. Whom will they give it to? Whom can they alert? Whom will that team of people alert? What could be the impact?

COACHING TIP: BUILD A TEAM

No matter what ALERT project the girls choose, guide them to keep their focus on not just what they themselves can do, but on what they can ALERT a team of others to try to do. That's how they can have more impact—and sustain the effort!

They might not have the time and resources to get a whole green roof built at their school, but by ALERTing others to the benefits of one, they might plant the seed of a plan with the school administration. That can lead to change down the road! That's what ALERTing is all about!

Inspiration, Please!

AT A GLANCE

Goal: With the ALERT issue established, girls get creative about reaching out to an Air Care Team and educating and inspiring that team to Act for Air. Along the way, girls consider the special flair they each can contribute to the team effort.

- Opening Ceremony: An Airy Mood

- Sounding the Call: What's the Plan?

- Adding Our Flair

- The Power of Pithiness

- Closing Ceremony

MATERIALS

- **Opening Ceremony:** girls' books.

- **Sounding the Call:** large sheet of papers and pens.

- A computer or other devices, if possible, for online searching.

PREPARE AHEAD

Now that girls have chosen an ALERT project, they will plan it out using all their creative flair! As the project unfolds, remember, it is not just the end result of the ALERT effort that matters. It is what girls can experience and learn as they strive to create change that will stick with them long past this one project. Here are a few questions to ask yourself as you guide a great ALERT experience:

- What opportunities have the girls had to ask others to Take Action?

- Whom have the girls met and interacted with? Has their network expanded?

- What have the girls learned about "alerting" others to a specific issue and asking for action on it?

- No matter what the specific results are of the ALERT effort, how will the girls know that their effort is important?

- What have the girls learned about working as a team?

AS GIRLS ARRIVE

Chat with any assistants about their roles before and during the gathering.

Opening Ceremony: An Airy Mood

Ask the girls how they would like to get themselves in an "airy" mood today. They might have their own ideas! If not, offer them these options to get them thinking:

- *If you can go outside (even just for a few minutes), breathe and engage all your senses. What do you see, hear, taste, and smell? Can you touch anything in the air? Maybe air is touching you! When you come in, take a minute and add it to your logs. Compare notes!*

- *Enjoy five minutes of silence together, maybe by looking into a candle's flame or at a photo of nature.*

- *As a group, look at the words of the Girl Scout Law (on the inside back cover of the girls' book and the inside front cover of this guide). Talk about the lines that you are involved with together on this journey.*

- *Spend a few minutes "upping your endorphins." Dance, climb up and down steps, or do some other active thing that is possible where you gather. Feeling breathless? Check page 85 of your book (the girls' book). Are you interested in making more time for cardio when we gather or between gatherings?*

CHOOSING THE ISSUE

If the girls haven't decided on their air issue yet, invite them to revisit the top two or three issues that surfaced in the previous session. Say: *Now that you've had time to think this through, how would you like to resolve this and decide on one issue? Has anyone decided to withdraw or change her issue?*

Keep guiding the discussion until it's time to decide. Ask: *What method would you like to use to decide? A simple vote? A short further discussion to build consensus?* If they choose the latter, give the girls a time limit to arrive at a resolution, congratulating them when they do and encouraging those whose issue did not win to accept the decision and pitch in with ideas along the way.

Sounding the Call: What's the Plan?

Begin by encouraging the girls to recap where they left off the last time the team gathered. What was the vision statement? Is there still energy around it? Are there changes anyone wants to suggest?

Let the girls know that the next step is to identify the people they will organize to act on behalf of air. These people will become their Air Care Team. The girls need to think about the best way to organize and inspire the team to "sound the call" to action.

Guide the team to build this plan by addressing the "W" and "H" questions (who, what, when, where, why, and how). Ask for a volunteer to capture the highlights of the plan with you on a big piece of paper that will be your "map" for the next several gatherings along the journey.

WHO (IDENTIFYING THE AIR CARE TEAM)

- Who is affected by this issue?

- Who are the people who can make an impact to improve this issue?

- Who might have some information or expertise on this issue that we need?

- Invite the girls to think about who is most affected by the issue their project addresses. Ask: *Is it students? Their parents? Health care providers? Others?*

- As the girls try to define the people most affected, encourage them to think more broadly. Ask questions like: *If the students are affected by X, does that mean the teachers are, too? What about the principal? The staff? The rest of the school community?*

HOW

- How will we reach out and contact these people? Invite them to an event? Post fliers? Call and talk to them?

- How will we educate and inspire them about our issue?

The methods could be as simple as:

- A colorful and attractive flier that explains the rational for the change or project and how each person can contribute to the change. (Take care with paper use, though!)

- A Web page announced by an e-mail blast to the "identified who's."

- A newsletter article in the local PTA bulletin or the districtwide bulletin.

- An e-mail blast to all families in the school or district.

- An "unveiling" of a green-our-school tree, garden, or planting to kick off an ALERT request.

More ambitious methods involving launches might include:

- An Air Fair, workshop, panel discussion, or meeting during which the girls ask attendees to act for air.

- A short play dramatizing the issue that could tour elementary and middle schools and community centers.

- A Cadette-created video or public service announcement on cable television stations.

- A mascot and a Facebook page that presents ongoing information and answers questions about the proposed change.

WHAT

What do we want our Air Care Team to go on and do? What is the simplest and most direct and effective way to say this?

What can we do to engage the Air Care Team in understanding why this issue and what we are asking them to do are so important?

What can we do to engage their senses in the call to action? What sights might help? Sounds? What scents convey the importance of this effort? What could they taste or touch that would get them committed?

WHEN

When will we put our plan in motion?

When will we get ready for that?

COMPLETING THE PLAN

With the plan sketched out, go back over all the ideas with girls, adjusting as needed and adding in specifics about who will do what. Encourage the girls to reach out and contact some of the people needed. It's a great practice for starting a network that can later help them with jobs or college references!

Adding Our Flair

When the group has their basic plan in place, encourage girls to start thinking about the specific ways each will be involved. Does she want to use some flair she feels strong about? Take a chance on trying out a new avenue for her flair?

Depending on the plans in motion, you might ask questions like these:

- *Does someone with artistic interests want to make posters and design signs and invitations?*

- *Would someone like to make a PowerPoint presentation or put a short video together?*

- *Are there aspiring actors or dancers in the group who could put on a skit or dress up as a project mascot?*

- *Does someone's family own a restaurant or bakery that could supply refreshments? A nursery willing to donate plants?*

- *How will we engage people's senses? Could we use any of the experiments or activities that we have tried?*

Encourage each girl to volunteer with a skill, a contact, or a passion that will be a special contribution to the project.

The Power of Pithiness

Ask girls if they know what it means to be "pithy" (it means to state your message briefly). What pithy slogans or catch phrases are they aware of? Why does pithiness matter? Now, encourage the girls to spend some time thinking like advertising executives. What techniques are used in ads that have caught the girls' attention? Short, catchy phrases? Visuals? A jingle? What would fit on T-shirt or a bumper sticker?

Ask the girls:

- *How can you distill your basic message down to just a few words?*
- *How can you use rhymes or wordplay to make your message memorable ?*
- *How can you mix serious content with catchy wording, alertness with fun?*

If your group is large, divide the girls into three or four groups and give them 10 minutes to brainstorm a catchy phrase or title for the project and its call to action.

When they return to the group, ask each team to present its idea and invite the group to reach a decision on which they like best. Say: *Could you use one phrase to reach parents and teachers, and another for students? Or is there a clear favorite?*

Encourage the team to incorporate their creativity into their plan.

Closing Ceremony

Invite the girls to share their hopes for their work to educate and inspire an Air Care Team.

Say: *We could just think of something we could do for air on our own. Why is it better to educate and inspire others to act, too? What do you hope our ALERT will accomplish?*

SAMPLE SESSION 7
ALERT! It's Happening!

AT A GLANCE

Goal: Girls continue planning and carrying out their ALERT efforts, concentrating on working as a team to mobilize their Air Care Team to act for air.

- ALERT Options
- Coaching Tips for the ALERT Project
- Team Check Suggestions

MATERIALS

- Paper and pens; the girls' books.
- The ALERT plan.
- Other materials determined by the specifics of the girls' vision.

PREPARE AHEAD

- The specifics of the plan the girls are putting in motion will guide what they do at this gathering—and the next few, if they are taking more time to ALERT. The notes and tips in this session design will help you continue to coach girls on their teamwork and planning skills to carry out the ALERT. You may find it useful to keep the project possibilities detailed throughout the girls' journey book handy, too!

- Whether the team is busy with the ALERT or pursuing other air-inspired interests, encourage the girls to continue taking a few minutes at the opening and closing of their gatherings to connect with one another, celebrate their time on this journey as special and distinct from their daily lives, and reflect on all the ways they are learning and growing as individuals and as a team.

AS GIRLS ARRIVE

Chat with any assistants about their roles before and during the gathering.

ALERT Options

At this and upcoming gatherings, depending on the issue, the time available, and the scope of the project the girls have chosen, the team may choose to:

- Use more time to plan and carry out the ALERT.

- Conduct an ALERT that requires less time—or perhaps even occurs during the school day or between gatherings—and use these team meetings to rally together on progress, next steps, etc.

- Visit or bring in guest experts on various air topics, related either to the ALERT project or other issues of interest the girls have identified from their book or research. Perhaps, for example, they want to know about public health efforts underway in their area to reduce smoking.

- Rehearse or prepare some of the ways the girls have come up with to engage others (mascot, video, music, pithy speaking points).

- Research information and possible actions for their chosen issue.

PERSONAL SPACE AND ENRICHMENT OPTIONS

If the girls on the team have become interested in exploring nature sounds and scents, or the science of air, or are enjoying quiet time or the "Need Some Space?" suggestions in their books, you can work with the team to structure meetings or add time or sessions to continue pursuing these kinds of activities as well. And if the girls are not interested in earning their ALERT Award, you can partner with them to make a whole journey out of these more-personal opportunities to create some "breathing room" in their lives!

Continue making the most of experts available locally to share aromatherapy, breathing exercises, cardio exercise, outdoor nature hikes and explorations, and even cooking skills (soufflé, anyone? Angel food cake, or some other light and airy treats?). And whenever the girls meet someone new, they can take time to find out what she studied, how she got interested in her career or hobby, and what else she suggests the girls explore. Remember, your local yoga expert might also have some good tips about running a business!

OPENING AND CLOSING CEREMONY SUGGESTIONS

Here are some suggestions, depending on the girls' interests:

- Continue the practice of silent time (aided by a candle or a nature photo).

- Reflect on specific lines of the Girl Scout Law and what they mean to the girls as they strive to make a difference in the world via their ALERT effort.

- Invite the girls to take turns bringing in songs whose lyrics inspire them to care for the Earth or one another.

- Check the air (both indoors and out) and compare notes. What is it important to always be aware of?

Coaching Tips for the ALERT Project

SUSTAINABILITY

As the ALERT effort progresses, continue asking questions that guide girls to think about sustainability:

- *How can those you educate and inspire (the Air Care Team) carry the project forward even if you are no longer around? How could Air Care Team members go on to educate and inspire others and keep "passing the action" forward?*

- *How can you partner with another organization to keep the work going after you finish?*

- *How could periodic "milestone" events, such as an annual Air Fair sponsored by a community or school, keep the ball rolling?*

PERSISTENCE!

Because many environmental issues are so big, the girls may sometimes feel that there is not a lot they can do to change things—and they might encounter this attitude in others, too, and get discouraged.

Encourage the girls to persevere. What examples of people who persevered despite the odds are they AWARE of? Remind the girls that although change may come slowly sometimes, even being part of a small snowball is important!

Guide the girls to be imaginative about how they use what they have learned—and all their senses—to break through the resistance they may encounter in others. If people are more AWARE, they may care!

TAILOR THE MESSAGE

Continue to ask the girls to think about how their favorite advertisements get their attention. Is it emphasis on a visual image with a short message? A direct statement? Something funny? How might they use these tactics to inspire others to get AWARE and ALERT? How do the tactics need to change depending on whom they are trying to reach?

Here are a few examples:

- Students and teachers may be affected by the unhealthy air in a building, so how do you get them to care? Could you get some of the best artists in your group to make funny signs to place in areas where the air is the worst? Could they use cartoon figures or even a mascot to draw attention to the poor air quality? Would a teacher let you put the signs facing outward in classroom windows nearest the bus stop?

- If you get your fellow students interested in the problem, could you create a different way of connecting with other students? Could you use humor more effectively with them than persuasion?

- How can you cut through the resistance of a busy principal, or parents, or a community that may not want to spend money on the problem?

- Who else might be an ally to help you break through resistance? A medical professional or another expert?

SPREADING THE WORD

Some of the methods for sounding the call (video, Facebook page, e-mail blasts) may overlap or replace the need for publicity.

But if there is a kickoff event or unveiling, such as a fair or AWAREness Day, the girls will want to work extra hard to get the word out so that attendance is good and they can see and feel the impact their efforts have.

Guide a discussion about publicity by saying something like: *Now that you have a catchy phrase and a good air project and a kickoff, where and how will you spread the word?*

Remind the girls that their goal is to engage others. Say: *You may find out about events from text messages, but you'll have to find different methods to connect with more people. What about . . .*

- a community radio station
- a community events listing in the newspaper

- your town's Web site

- a PTA bulletin

- a Facebook page for your project

If they girls are stumped, say things like: *Remember whom you are trying to reach. Do they respond best to:*

- e-mail blasts

- colorful fliers (be careful about wasting paper, though!)

- mascots parading around town, on the campus, or through the mall

- videos shown with morning announcements at school

- newspaper articles and events listings

- some combination of the above

PLANNING AND CONDUCTING A MEETING, AIR FAIR, OR KICKOFF EVENT

Encourage the girls to review "Tips for Success in the Air" (page 108) before launching their project to their Air Care Team. Then get them thinking about these pointers, too:

- Set goals. *What are the ideas and issues you want to air? What do you want people to feel? How can you use the launch to issue your call for action and get people excited about it?*

- Decide how to open the meeting or event or video. *How can you get people's attention right from the start? How can you inspire them to want to participate?*

- Decide how to guide a discussion, moderate a panel, or solicit feedback. *Will you need an expert or two on hand to keep the meeting on track, solicit comments, and/or answer questions about your issue?*

- Think about when and how during the launch your team can sound the ALERT and issue the call to action. *Do you want to have pledge cards so those you inspire will make a promise to follow though on what you're asking them to do? Will there be a call-back number on a public service announcement? An e-mail address?*

- Think about how to record the insights and results of the launch and gather contact information for further follow-up. *Do you want to use a tape recorder? A video camera? Take notes? Do you want to have a sign-in sheet so that people can leave their e-mail addresses?*

- Decide how you want people to join you in taking action. *New ideas may come up along the way. But be sure you have any fliers, fact sheets, tip sheets, and lists of Web sites or related events ready to distribute as participants leave. That way they'll have the tools they need to support your project to clear the air.*

Whatever you do, be mindful of how you use paper, and how you hand it out, too. You'll want to model great and innovative ways to provide information without wasting paper.

Also, remind the girls that the "one-time event" is not the end of their ALERT. You might say: *A meeting, kickoff, or fair is a great way to sound the ALERT and get people engaged. But what will you ask people to do? And how can you follow up to make sure you really make an impact with your air issue?*

Team Check

Guide the girls to consider how they have been working as a team. Ask questions like these:

How are we doing on being open-minded? Do we accept opinions that are different from our own?

How can the team do a better job of including everyone?

Are we addressing conflicts and disagreements fairly? How?

How is our communication? Honest and open?

Encourage the girls to list two or three ways that they are doing well as a team and two or three ways that they commit to improving upon.

SAMPLE SESSION 8
Take the Pulse

AT A GLANCE

Goal: Girls earn the ALERT Award and follow up on their effort to assess what "care for air" they may have set in motion. They decide if there are other actions they or their Air Care Team can do to boost the effort. They begin to think about how they will AFFIRM and pass on their efforts as leaders, and take some Air Time to do an activity of their choosing.

- Opening Ceremony: Earning ALERT
- Pulse Check: Toward AFFIRM
- Giving Thanks
- Gathering AFFIRMations
- Air TIme Options
- Closing Ceremony: Around the World

MATERIALS

- Opening Ceremony: ALERT Awards; paper, pens, and markers.
- The girls' book.
- Materials for thank you notes.

PREPARE AHEAD

- Depending on the kind of ALERT project the girls have created and the time available to the team, the girls may still be up to their elbows in carrying out the ALERT. That's fine! Just come to this session's ideas when the team is ready to earn their ALERT Award and start AFFIRMing their impact!

- During this session, you will present girls with their ALERT Awards. Think ahead of time about some great examples of their efforts that you can highlight as you give out the awards. Check out the ideas on page 84 of this guide as a starting point.

- If appropriate, perhaps a few members of the Air Care Team who assisted with or witnessed the girls' efforts would like to participate in the award ceremony, too!

- During this session, you will also guide girls to find signs of their impact (AFFIRMations) and to think of a creative way to collect and present them for your next gathering. Ultimately, the Cadettes will give their AFFIRMation collage to a team of Girl Scout Juniors to inspire them to come along on a *Breathe* journey and create their own "airwaves" when they become Cadettes.

AS GIRLS ARRIVE

Chat with any assistants about who will do what before and during the gathering.

Opening Ceremony: Earning ALERT

Write this quote from inspirational former first lady Rosalynn Carter where all the girls can see it.

"A leader takes people where they want to go. A great leader takes people where they don't necessarily want to go but ought to be."

Engage the girls in a discussion by asking questions like: *Based on your own effort to ALERT, what do you think about this statement? Why does the world need leaders? How do your AWARE and ALERT efforts make you a leader? What is your own special leadership flair?*

Award each girl her ALERT Award, congratulating girls individually and as a team for demonstrating leadership.

COACHING TIP: FINDING THE AFFIRMATIVES!

Not all projects will result in an immediate, observable difference! Guide girls to feel positive about their effort by understanding that it may set off small changes that will soon snowball.

For example, perhaps girls spoke with a parent association and school principal about starting a green roof. For budgetary or logistical reasons this project is not possible right now. Still, the parents and school staff learned things that made them more AWARE. Have they agreed to a smaller project? More plants? A new tree or two? Every action matters!

Can a few parents who heard the presentation provide a note about what they learned and how they might incorporate it into a change in their own life? Have they passed the ALERT on to someone else?

Gathering even a little evidence of the results of their effort to educate and inspire others will show girls that they have had a positive impact! That feeling is so important because it can propel girls to keep on striving to change the world!

Now is a good time to give the girls some specific examples of what you observed about their efforts. Here are a few examples. Maybe you saw girls:

- speak up even if nervous
- stick with it after a disappointment
- develop an especially creative idea
- work through a conflict together
- organize themselves
- apply some information they learned to educate others

Ask questions like: *What part of your plan worked really well? What interested people the most? How willing were people to take action? How does it feel to try to influence others? What would you do differently?*

Pulse Check: Toward AFFIRM

Now that the girls have sounded the ALERT, encourage them to consider what they accomplished, what they learned, and what they might do differently next time.

Next, get a discussion going about anything the girls want to do to keep the project moving forward, striving to make the change ongoing and sustainable. Depending on the time and commitment possible, offer ideas like:

- A monthly checkup on the change.
- An annual event reminding the community to keep efforts going.
- Asking a different organization—school PTA or foundation, American Lung Association—to take over the project or just one aspect of it.

Pulse Check: Teamwork

Ask the girls to make a list of the biggest challenges they faced as a team. Say: *Were the challenges among yourselves or were they out in the world you were trying to influence?*

Next to each item on the list, ask the girls to write how they were able to confront and surmount the challenge by working as a team. What grade would girls give their teamwork? As a team, what would they try to improve?

Conclude with a discussion that answers this question: *What do you think is the biggest value of teamwork?*

Giving Thanks

Ask girls to think back upon who the biggest helpers were along the ALERT airway. *Friends and families? Experts? Your principal? Who do you want to thank? How? Perhaps through a handmade note? Via e-mail? By inviting guests to the journey's closing ceremony?*

As the team plans to thank their supporters, you might also mention: Writing thank you's is not only being considerate; it's an important networking skill!

Gathering AFFIRMations

Say: *Affirm means "to declare with confidence." Are we confident that we have made some impact with our ALERT project? Whether it is big or small, what matters is that we are trying to make a difference. That's leadership! How can we check and find signs of our action?*

- *Is there evidence that your actions have led to progress or even a solution to your air issue? How can you document it? Depending on the project, perhaps there is a visual sign of improvement? A new scent in the air (or less of a yucky one)? Less noise? More people working toward change?*

- *Have you heard from the people you influenced? Are they making comments or sending messages back about your action? Are you getting thank you notes? E-mails? Newspaper mentions?*

Ask the girls how they want to creatively collect and organize evidence of their ALERT project. Can they:

- *Contact their Air Care Team and ask how it is taking up the call to action?*

- *Review the "pledge" cards or sign-up list from the ALERT effort and see if some follow-up idea emerges?*

Ask the team to work toward gathering the "evidence" between now and the next session. Can each girl or pair commit to bringing some evidence?

Also ask the team to decide how they would like to organize the signs of their impact—perhaps in a scrapbook, a PowerPoint presentation, or a special *Breathe* box? Maybe they want to attach the evidence—collage-like—right to their plan and put it on poster boards?

The team can also consider how they will add evidence of their teamwork. Photos? Flair moments in a poem?

SIGNS OF AFFIRMATION

Depending on the project, signs of progress may be possible via:

- word-of-mouth comments written down and summarized

- letters from people involved

- before-and-after photos of a problem mitigated and the people affected

- a list of signatures of people who promised to take your action, too

- a report in the school or PTA bulletin

- a community news article about the project

- thank you notes from those who have experienced improvement

Let the girls know that at the next gathering they will assemble their AFFIRMation collage to present to a team of Girl Scout Juniors as an inspiration to try the *Breathe* journey when they become Cadettes. The more girls start acting for air, the bigger the ultimate impact!

Find out if any of the girls know teams of Girl Scout Juniors whom they would like to give their AFFIRMation collage to. Maybe someone can volunteer to network via school, a place of worship, or your Girl Scout council?

Air Time Options

As the *Breathe* journey winds down, encourage the girls to take another pass through their book. You might ask: *What would you like to spend a little time doing or talking about together before the journey ends? As a whole team or in mini-teams, choose a topic and get to it!*

Consider, too, revisiting something you found interesting in an earlier gathering and want to do more of, whether it is science experiments, making an airy treat, "tuning in," or enjoying silence (or blare!) together. You can start one or more of these activities today and then finish them up at the next gathering.

Here are some examples to share with the girls:

- *"THINK LIKE AN ENGINEER," on page 19 of your book, invites you to think of a gadget that has not yet been invented and design it. How about designing a gadget that does something for or related to air?*

- *Notice all the wordplay on air throughout your book. "Armchair quarterback" is discussed on page 34, "Hares, Mares, Bears" is on page 62, and mentions of prepare, flair, éclair, and AWARE appear throughout the book. What fun with words might you like to have? Create a group poem in which everyone adds a line ending with an "air sound"? Everyone write down all the words they can think of that have an "air" sound and see who has the most?*

- *Say: Try the exercise on page 79 of your book to convince people not to smoke! Practice your reasons on each other!*

- *Check out the list of interesting airy careers on page 98 of your book. Which have you never thought about doing? Why not? Which might you start to think about now?*

Closing Ceremony: Around the World

Gather the team in and say: *All over Earth, people share the same air. As we go around our circle, say where you would like the air you are breathing to go next—and what you would like to do if you went with it!*

SAMPLE SESSION 9
Signs of AFFIRMation

AT A GLANCE

Goal: Girls affirm their impact on Earth's air, compiling their AFFIRMation collage to present to Girl Scout Juniors. They also wrap up their "Air Time" fun and plan the closing celebration for their *Breathe* Journey.

- **Opening Ceremony: AFFIRM**
- **Earning AFFIRM**
- **Air Time**
- **Planning a Final Celebration**

MATERIALS

- Opening Supplies needed to present the AFFIRMations girls have gathered according to their plans (scrapbook, PowerPoint presentation, posters, photos, etc.).

- Notecard or blank paper for a note to Girl Scout Juniors.

- Supplies needed for any "Air Time" fun begun at the last gathering.

- AFFIRM Awards.

PREPARE AHEAD

- Try to follow up with the girls between sessions so that each girl comes with the "affirmation" she agreed to track down and share as well as any supplies she can share for the team's AFFIRMation collage.

- Also reach out to a few of the people involved in the Air Care Team the girls organized. Ask them for a comment, note, or other AFFIRMation of progress that you might be able to contribute to the collection the girls are gathering.

- If the girls did not decide on the younger girls to give their compiled AFFIRMations to, network in your Girl Scout community and see if you can identify a group of Girl Scout Juniors who have not yet received a gift from other Cadettes. Ask your council. Perhaps some (or all) of this younger group of Girl Scouts can participate in part of the next session? Or the girls can make arrangements to "gift" their AFFIRMations to the younger girls behind the scenes.

AS GIRLS ARRIVE

Talk with any assistants about their roles before and during the gathering.

Opening Ceremony: AFFIRM

Gather the girls into a circle and invite them (individually or in small teams) to report back on their investigation of how their ALERT project had an impact. As girls share these AFFIRMations, they can add the comments, letters, or photos to the team's collage (in a scrapbook or box, on a poster board, etc.).

Guide girls who need assistance to think of and capture in some way (their own note on paper, perhaps) a sign of their impact. An AFFIRMation can be as simple as stating, "Six more people now know something new about caring for air!" or "We are working to get a quiet zone set up in school."

Once all the girls have added a sign of impact to the compilation, encourage them to make a simple team note to the younger Girl Scouts they will give their AFFIRMation collage to. The note could mention points like:

- We are glad we did the "XYZ" Alert effort because we learned
  _____.

- We know we made a difference because
  _____.

- We are presenting you with our collection of AFFIRMations because we want to inspire you!

- When you are a Cadette, try to take action for Earth's air, too! Earth needs all of us because
  _____.

- Maybe you'll get an idea from us . . . but add your own unique flair, too!

- We are counting on you!

Earning AFFIRM

With the AFFIRMation collage complete, present the AFFIRM Award to the girls! Let them know that whenever they look at it, it can be a powerful reminder that they have the power to make a difference in their world!

Air Time

If the team started or planned an "air time" fun activity at the last gathering, now is the time to get to it and air it up!

Planning a Final Celebration

Ask the girls who they would like to include in their closing gathering and what tone they would like it to have. Is the closing:

- Just for them! A chance to have a blast?

- A more formal ceremony with guests? A chance to showcase all they have learned and accomplished?

- A chance to network again with the Air Care Team and give thanks?

- A special outing or trip—maybe one the girls have been planning all along?

- A day (or afternoon or evening) outdoors enjoying air?

- Something else?

Based on the team's preferences, guide the girls to organize the journey's closing gathering. Perhaps they can think of ways to ensure that the closing invigorates all their senses:

Sound: Will they enjoy silence together? Invite guests to try it? Hear inspiring music? The sounds of nature? A little of each?

Smell: What scenty stuff will lift the spirits?

Sight: Breathtaking photos of Earth—and the Cadette team in action, perhaps?

Taste: Anything with whipped cream (air's in there!), meringues (or lemon meringue pie), popovers, cheese soufflé, air-popped corn (sprinkled with . . .), bubbly seltzer with fruit afloat . . .

Touch: Would girls like to blow bubbles (or dandelions), or pinwheels, let the air out of balloons, or do some other crazy little thing that lets them feel the air while they let go of their cares?

SAMPLE SESSION 10
Up, Up, and Away!

AT A GLANCE

Goal: Girls celebrate their accomplishments on this journey and reflect on their roles as heirs apparent of air and all of Earth's elements.

- **Celebrate with Purpose**
- **Your Now and Future Air**

MATERIALS

- Whatever supplies are needed based upon the plans the girls have made.

PREPARE AHEAD

- Get in the spirit of the journey closing by reading over the introduction and conclusion of the girls' book.

- Try to contact the girls and the Friends and Family Network, reminding everyone about what they promised to share or do for the closing celebration (provide transportation for an outing, help with refreshments or other supplies, etc.).

AS GIRLS ARRIVE

Talk with any assistants about their roles before and during the celebration.

Celebrate with Purpose!

Enjoy whatever activities or discussions the team has planned! Whether the team is outdoors or indoors, alone or with guests, encourage a few last moments (on this journey!) for girls to *Breathe* in the purpose of all they have learned and experienced.

HEIR APPARENT REFLECTION

Consider encouraging each girl to reflect on the journey and share her thoughts as she claims her space as an Heir Apparent of Air (and all Earth's Elements). Girls can take a few moments alone to think about the insights they have gained and then share their thoughts with one another. You might use the Heir Apparent reflection on the next page as a guide. The girls can each have their own copy of it (or make their own on recycled paper!) and then place it in their book.

CLOSING CEREMONY IDEAS

The end of this *Breathe* journey can be marked as a special event by any ceremony of the girls' choosing or such airy traditions as:

- lighting an aromatic candle and joining hands in a circle
- silent time as the girls once again become aware of life-giving oxygen going in and out of their lungs
- going outdoors to let kites play in the wind
- visiting a favorite wind spot

If the girls choose to fly kites, perhaps they'd like to make their own out of recycled materials. How about kites made of plastic grocery bags, inspired by those of artist Miwa Koizumi, featured on pages 100–101 of the girls' book?

I Am
an Heir Apparent of Air
(and All of Earth's
Elements)

What that means to me is _____

_____.

I will try to keep using my special flair for _____

to _____.

As I became AWARE of _____,

I also discovered that I value _____.

By working to sound the ALERT for air, I connected with others too.

Teamwork has taught me _____

_____.

And, in taking action for Earth's air,

I can definitely AFFIRM that I _____

_____.

Your Now and Future Air

Before the celebration ends, encourage the girls to check out all the opportunities available to them in Girl Scouts. Let them know who they can talk to at their Girl Scout council to pursue them!

They might, for example, want to:

- Earn the Girl Scout Silver Award

- Go camping or to camp

- Check out another leadership journey

- Be in a troop (or keep one going)

- Earn a LiA (Leader in Action) by assisting with Brownie journeys

- Participate in special events

- Travel

If any Cadettes are bridging to Girl Scout Seniors next year, they might want to get a taste—literally—of *Sow What?*, the It's Your Planet--Love It! leadership journey for Seniors. Perhaps they can locate a Senior group that might join their *Breathe* celebration and share some *Sow What?* snacks along with highlights of what they enjoyed along this leadership journey, which is focused on food and land issues, and the global reach of our food networks.

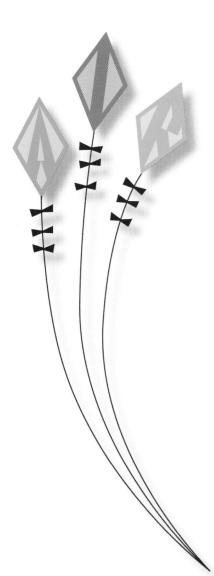

AIRY THOUGHTS FROM THE ARCHIVES

No matter how the Cadettes choose to celebrate *Breathe*, they might enjoying hearing some air-inspiring passages from the early days of Girl Scouting. The following passages come from *How Girls Can Help Their Country: The 1913 Handbook for Girl Scouts.* While you're sharing them, encourage the girls to consider how some things have changed and some haven't!

Here's a passage about noise:

> We can all help by being considerate. Don't shout near hospitals or churches, and stop any noise where there is illness, be quiet where children are being got to sleep, and be careful not to start nervous horses. Show that you are thinking of others, so that it will be a good example to passersby.

And one about smoking:

> Some girls think it a fine thing to smoke and start it without thinking. But it is only a silly habit and by the time they have found out this they find it hard to drop.

And you might remind the girls of these wonderful air lines, also from *How Girls Can Help Their Country*, which are also featured on page 9 of their book.

> Fresh air is your great friend . . . Open all your windows as often as you can.

Encourage them to remember that wherever they might soar in life.

Breathe

Congratulations to you! You have guided girls on a breathtaking journey. Take a moment and reflect on your experience, too!

What have you discovered about yourself?
Your values related to the Earth?

_____

_____

_____

How have you connected with Cadettes? Community members?
How do these connections make you feel?

_____

_____

_____

What impact has your own Take Action (as a Girl Scout volunteer)
had on the girls? Your community? The world?!

_____

_____

_____

Now that you have learned all this, what will you do next?

_____

_____

_____